Hanged If You Do ...

Disclaimer

The identities of children, young people and families have been changed and pseudonyms have been used. Case details have also been modified to further protect their anonymity and confidentiality. To any colleagues who regret that I didn't do the same for them – sorry!

Hanged If You Do ...

Reflections from a Career in Child Protection

Paul Harrison

ORPEN PRESS

Published by
Orpen Press
Upper Floor, Unit B3
Hume Centre
Hume Avenue
Park West Industrial Estate
Dublin 12

email: info@orpenpress.com
www.orpenpress.com

Paperback ISBN 978-1-78605-116-5
ePub ISBN 978-1-78605-117-2

Printed in Dublin by SPRINTprint Ltd

'Come away, O human child!
To the waters and the wild
With a faery, hand in hand,
For the world's more full of weeping than you can
understand.'
W.B. Yeats, 'The Stolen Child'

Acknowledgments

A couple of years ago I was chatting with Professor Robbie Gilligan in Trinity College Dublin, who asked me if I'd ever considered writing a memoir. I had, but I hadn't done anything about it – so thanks for the prompt Robbie. I'm grateful to Ivy Bannister, whose memoir course in the Irish Writers' Centre was a big help – and to her 'class of 2017' for setting high standards in a supportive environment. Thanks to Mary Ahern, Dr Helen Buckley and Norah Gibbons for reading drafts and providing honest feedback. Norah, who died before the book was published, was a fearless champion for children and a great colleague whom I miss.

I am grateful to Gerry O'Neill for his guidance and to Kieran McGrath for filling in those memory gaps. Thanks to Stephanie McCarthy for keeping me on the straight and narrow and to Ann McWilliams, whose own work prompted the idea for the book title. I recall with particular gratitude the late Noreen Kearney, my former tutor in Trinity College Dublin, who first led me onto the yellow brick road of research.

Thanks to all those I worked with and from whom I learned so much. I hope the book provides some insight into the tribulations of working in child protection, but also into some of the rewards for those who can stick with it.

I am especially grateful to all at Orpen Press for running with my proposal and seeing it through so expertly to publication.

Lastly, my thoughts are with the children, young people and families I have worked with and for over the past four decades. I was never perfect, I was sometimes wrong, but I hope most of what I did was of benefit to them in the long run.

For Mary,
who barely gets a mention in the book but who was right
beside me throughout my career

Contents

Introduction

C hild protection social workers have to walk a very narrow line between protecting children in their families and protecting them from their families. Well documented scandals have involved the failures of social workers to intervene soon enough, if at all, and failures involving premature or draconian interventions which were subsequently found to be unwarranted. While doctors differ and patients die, there is a public expectation that social workers will protect all of the children all of the time.

In applying Solomon's wisdom to such cases, I had to determine, on the balance of probability, if the forcible removal of a child from his or her family was the lesser of two evils. The first was to leave the child in a dangerous situation, where their health or wellbeing was likely to be permanently impaired. The second was to remove them from the danger, in the knowledge that this too would cause lasting psychological damage to the child and other family members.

Nothing in my social work training adequately prepared me for the events that still slip into my dreams decades later. I started out with virtuous and altruistic notions of helping people. This fits with a common stereotype of social workers – men in open-toe sandals who bring their pets to work, and women in home-knitted cardigans with a knot of tissue stuck up the sleeve. When I was applying for a place on a social work training course in 1976, I had to write an essay on 'Social Work

- and why I want to do it'. This is a flavour of what I came up with: 'I have never considered social work as being able to move humanity forward. That is for scientists and statesmen. I see social workers as shepherding people who have been left behind. Social work is helping people to help themselves.' This, plus an interview, and I was in.

While on a student placement, I helped an elderly couple whose son was a long-stay patient in a psychiatric hospital. In gratitude they presented me with a box of handkerchiefs. I was living the dream. Now, four decades and no presents later, I look back on a career in which I was spat upon, threatened and assaulted; libelled, slandered and sued; stalked, cursed and bribed; maligned by the media and denigrated in the Dáil. So much for the warm glow of benevolent do-gooding.

Looking back now, even though I have spent most of my career in management, it is the individual cases I remember most vividly. But management too is not without drama and it would not be possible for me to write a memoir without recounting some of those cliffhanging moments. At the end of the day, social work practice and management is all about human relationships. This is my account of those relationships over the past forty years in the toughest and most emotive social work environments of them all - child protection.

1

NAI

'*D*o you want to hold the baby?', the nurse asked me. I didn't want to, but I could hardly say no. I held out my arms and she handed her to me. All wrapped in pink, she was as fragrant and delicate as a rosebud. Now I was glad she was in my arms. She wasn't cold, having been laid out in the warmth of the mortuary chapel. I kissed her forehead just above the contusion that the mortician couldn't disguise. The bruising was covered with make-up but the lump stuck out like a blot upon her pale, white skin. A palpable mass, the autopsy report would later describe it.

I tried not to be emotional. But what is the point of human services if you can't mourn the sudden death of a little baby? 'I know', the nurse said, rubbing my arm, and we just sat there. I grieved for the baby whom I had known for each of her six months of life. And I worried for myself, guilty that I hadn't foreseen this and troubled about the consequences. Someone had killed this child. Non-Accidental Injury (NAI).

*

In college, we studied the early works of Hefner and Kemp in the USA relating to the battered child. And I still have my original copy of *Child Abuse* by Kemp and Kemp. On the cover is a boy with a bruised face and the classic expression of frozen watchfulness – that learned behaviour of the child who knows better than to cry.

The framing of child abuse as a social problem, in this part of the world, was attributable in large measure to the death of Maria Colwell in England in 1973. Aged eight years, she was battered to death by her stepfather and, at the post-mortem, was found to be significantly malnourished and underweight. She had spent a considerable amount of her short life in foster care. Several reports had been made to social services by teachers and neighbours, and she had been visited at home by a succession of different social workers.

The case provoked a national scandal where the role of social work in families was questioned. Social policy shifted from perceiving certain families in terms of deprivation, which needed to be relieved, to deviancy and inadequacy, which required state intervention and control. A new public expectation of social work emerged whereby state social services should identify children at risk and protect them from harm. All of them. Always. Social service departments began to prioritise NAI for fear another Maria Colwell would land on their desks.

In Ireland in the early 1970s, many of the senior social workers had come home from the UK to develop community-based social work teams within the newly established health boards. Influenced by the fallout of the Colwell scandal, the new senior social workers prioritised non-accidental injury. Until then child protection had been the domain of the Irish Society for the Prevention of Cruelty to Children (ISPCC), whose inspectors visited families and had the power to bring parents to court. These so-called 'cruelty men' had been a feature of Irish society since the nineteenth century. However, with the development of community-based social work teams, the ISPCC had a rethink and directed itself away from child protection and towards primary prevention through community-based family centres.

Statutory child protection had arrived and from the mid-1970s to the early 1980s NAI to children was a social work

Hanged If You Do...

preoccupation. We searched it out like hounds let loose, even though the prevalence was low. In 1978, when I started, 243 cases of NAI were reported nationally for all of that year and most of the preceding year. In 2018, child protection referrals to the Child and Family Agency were running at up to 5,000 cases per month.

In college, the theory of social work had taught me the principles of client self-determination, acceptance and a non-judgemental attitude. The contrast between college theory and working reality was stark. Back then there was no induction programme for new staff starting off in the health board system. You were shown the ropes by more senior colleagues, who all seemed fierce and ruthless to me. From the get-go, I learned that in the real world of child protection, parents were seen as suspects and you found out bad things about them. No practical assistance or supportive intervention was offered. Around that time, the American television series *Hill Street Blues* was popular. It featured tough cops in a downtown city station fighting crime and living hard. They knew all the theory, but they also knew what worked. The social work team related so much to this kick-ass series that they even assigned the names of the television characters to individual members of staff.

Procedurally, if it looked like we were making it up as we went along it was because we were. The first guidance, provided by the Department of Health, was the *Memorandum on NAI to Children* in 1977. It was medically focused with an emphasis on clinical identification. Responsibility was given to health boards to coordinate notifications of NAI and, within health boards, the responsibility fell to the director of community care, who had to be a medical doctor. The rest of us were told in the guidance that where our suspicions were aroused, our objective should be to get the child to a doctor for examination as soon as possible. Because doctor knows best.

If all the children who were reported as being, or suspected of being, abused were taken into care Ireland would have to open up care facilities of internment camp proportions. But emerging Irish social policy positioned social work in the community and not in the big institutions which were starting to close down. Of course, not all NAI cases ended in death or even serious injury. There was a spectrum of abuse that had to be assessed and these would test the wisdom of Solomon himself.

The *Memorandum on NAI* advised us that the first signs may be very slight, giving the example of a minor injury such as a bruise. So it was that I got a call from St Vincent's School in North William Street, run by the Daughters of Charity. The nuns once ran an orphanage from that site and there was still a children's home on the premises. A little girl, aged eight, had come to school very upset and sobbing. One cheek was pock-marked and flaming red. When asked what was wrong, she told her teacher that her mother hit her on the way out to school.

I called to the flat when the child was still in class. The mother answered the door. She wasn't much more than a girl herself. When I told her why I was there and asked for an explanation she dissolved into a sobbing child and told me that she had done it. She was brushing her daughter's hair on her way out to school, but the child was wriggling and resisting. In a flash of exasperation, she struck the child with the brush on the face and pushed her out the hall door to school.

The backstory followed easily now that the truth was out. Her boyfriend had just split up with her. He often helped with the rent, which was now overdue. This was Tuesday, she had a tenpenny piece in her purse until payday on Thursday, and she had just sent the child off to school with the last scraping of bread and jam. Now, in addition to her relationship and money problems, she was mortified by guilt and remorse. I gave her a few bob from my pocket and a note for the community welfare officer to help her out with the rent. Case closed.

*

Deeply embedded in the social work psyche back then was a dislike and mistrust of public health nurses. As part of my socialisation into my first social work team, I was encouraged to consider them as a sneaky lot. That was because they

Hanged If You Do...

referred every little tittle-tattle to social workers, then headed for the hills lest they be held in any way accountable for the risk. These 'baby nurses' were midwives as well as registered general nurses and, as such, were a lifesaver to inexperienced parents. They provided a unique universal service by visiting every newborn baby in their own home soon after discharge from the maternity hospital and at intervals thereafter. In that capacity they were well placed to see the baby in their own environment and to observe the family circumstances over time. The thing was, they wanted to maintain their congenial image as helpful and supportive local professionals. For this reason, they dodged attempts to share the monitoring of potential or actual risk within families and the social worker always ended up doing the dirty work.

Then, as now, the necessity for inter-professional cooper-ation to achieve good outcomes could be put to music. But sound theory can still be stymied when professionals become entrenched in their own particular bunker. In 1982 the Minister of Health, Dr Michael Woods, initiated an investigation into the circumstances surrounding the deaths of two children, known to the Eastern Health Board, who died of child abuse. It was the first such investigation of its kind and was conducted in a low-key manner that would be unheard of today. It concluded that the professionals had acted in a concerned and conscien-tious manner but that there had been a lack of coordinated effort. The Minister also emphasised the strong tradition of family life and the importance of keeping families together. After all, this principle was enshrined in the Constitution and there was little political or public appetite for interfering in family life.

*

It was the public health nurse who noticed there was some-thing wrong with the baby's leg. She was on a routine visit to a young single mother who recently had her first child. Arrangements were quickly made for the infant to be admitted to the Children's Hospital in Temple Street. It turned out that the baby boy had a fractured femur, and the mother had no explanation for it. On physical examination he was found to be well-nourished, otherwise unmarked and developmentally on target. Radiology showed up nothing except the one fracture. Frequently in NAI, imaging will show up older, perhaps mended, fractures of different ages.

The medical social worker was called in. The first enquiry usually involves cross-checking the type of injury against the presenting reason for admission. My wife and I, as the parents of young children, once found ourselves on the wrong side of hospital suspicion when we presented ourselves once too often at A&E in Temple Street. Our daughter, then aged about two, smashed a toothbrush glass from the bathroom, leaving shards of glass in her forehead. After various huddles between nursing and medical staff the medical social worker was called for. My wife and I were interviewed separately, having been given no opportunity to confer with each other beforehand. Fortunately, our stories lined up, our child was patched up and we were sent home with another story to add to our archive of family anecdotes.

But this young mother could give no account. She was as perplexed as the medical and nursing staff, and obviously concerned for her baby. According to my book by Kemp and Kemp, single parents are less likely to be abusive than couples. While this might seem counterintuitive, the theory is that couples in abusive families are not supportive of each other and compete for attention in order to have their own needs met. Abuse occurs when certain features are present. Often there will be a history of emotional or physical deprivation – and maybe abuse as well. The child will be seen as troublesome, unlovable or disappointing in some respect. There is usually a crisis point, such as a flare-up in the child's behaviour, or an external event bringing pressure on the family. Lastly, there is social isolation where the parent does not have a reliable lifeline to back-up and support at times of crisis.

The medical social worker and I talked with the mother, gathering a lot of background detail and her current circumstances. She had had a fairly deprived childhood but had come through it. The pregnancy was unplanned but she was obviously well attached to her son. She lived from hand to mouth on social welfare. The baby had been feeding but he not sleeping well. She was stressed out and had no immediate family or friends to turn to. When we got into the nitty-gritty of her daily routine, she was able to describe changing the baby's nappy at a time when she was jaded and he was crying. She roughly forced his legs out of the way and that was all it took.

At the case conference that followed, doctors agreed that this was the cause and it would therefore be classified as a non-accidental injury. Even the mother accepted the scenario, but she protested that she didn't mean to do it. She had inflicted the injury, but did so unintentionally. Nowadays there is a debate about the distinction between an inflicted injury that was unintentional and a non-accidental injury that was deliberate. It would also be possible to apply to the court for the baby to be made subject to a supervision order. In this way the baby could stay in the care of his mother but with certain conditions attached, such as agreeing to submit to medical examinations and allow access to the social worker and public health nurse whenever they called.

Back then in the late 1970s, working under the old British Children Act 1908, things were more black-and-white. We were faced with taking the baby into care or not. Solomon's sword was wielded at the case conference, splitting opinion in two. Do we play it safe and remove the child from future risk, or do we take the risk and support the mother-and-child relationship where an obvious bond existed? We took the risk, knowing too well what the consequences would be if we got it wrong.

The cases where parents or guardians are monstrous are actually the easy ones because there is no such dilemma. Another baby of a similar age, who was admitted to Temple Street around the same time, was found to have over twenty fractures of varying ages. The live-in boyfriend was the perpetrator. The child wasn't his and he resented his very existence. The fractures to the ribs were caused by squeezing. The ones to the limbs from lifting and throwing. He went to jail and the child was taken into care because his mother had to have known her child was in real danger. One night on the way home from work, a colleague was flicking channels on the car radio. There was a message from the mother to the prisoner: 'Miss you loads and can't wait for you to come home.'

*

Meanwhile I was sitting outside the mortuary chapel with a dead baby in my arms – bewildered that it had come to this. A hurriedly convened case conference was called to review all the facts. This had not been considered a high-risk case. It was referred to social work by the maternity hospital because the young mother was seen as vulnerable and in need of support. This was her first child. Her boyfriend was considered an asset because he agreed to move in with her prior to the birth. As parents they were immature and ill-equipped and, although clueless, were nevertheless charmed with the baby when she arrived. The public health nurse called often, as did I. Back then there wasn't much to offer by way of practical help – it was more a case of monitored encouragement.

When I heard from the children's hospital that the baby was admitted, in a coma with a suspected non-accidental injury, I was flabbergasted. There was nothing in the demeanour of either parent to suggest that they were particularly stressed or impatient with her. Both seemed devastated when their baby died soon after admission. The meeting concluded that the tragedy was unpredictable, which was a let-off for me. But the parents' accounts of events leading to the fatal injury didn't line up. The mother said she had left the flat to go shopping, leaving the father in charge. The father said he had come home to find the child unconscious and the mother shaking her and screaming that she had rolled off the sofa. Then, a few days after the incident, just as the Gardaí were preparing to interview him, the father took the ferry to Wales.

2

Child Protection Light

*I*n 1979, Guinness launched a new beer, Guinness Light. The slogan was, 'They said it couldn't be done.' It turns out they were right. The product flopped, and Guinness quickly reverted their attention to the full-bodied stuff that had been hitting the spot since 1759. Since statutory child protection services began to evolve in Ireland from the mid-1970s, social work assigned to itself the full-bodied responsibilities of investigating and intervening in cases of child abuse. But then in 1980, the final *Report of the Task Force on Child Care Services* was published. It declared that, heretofore, insufficient emphasis was placed on helping children in their families, as opposed to helping them after they had been removed. The concept of child welfare was introduced by the task force, which promoted the importance of prevention and early intervention. This evoked a dilemma for social work that rumbles on to this day. Will Child Protection Light ever catch on?

The task force was a Government-appointed working party. My first boss, Niav O'Daly, was a member – the only social worker and the only woman. I reported to her on a sunny June day in 1978 at her offices in Killarney Street at the Five Lamps. The Social Work Department was in a former health and dental clinic attached to a block of flats at St Joseph's Mansions. It was a bleak, heavily fortified building that repelled natural light as well as it did intruders. On the street outside, a group of teen-agers sat in the sun, their backs against the railings. With the hairstyle and ankle-flapping trousers of the Bay City Rollers, they drank beer from stubby brown bottles. I could feel them eying me suspiciously on my way in. Niav came out to greet me wearing a long flowing dress and sandals. Despite her casual appearance she had the clipped authority of a school principal. I soon learned that when she asked you, 'how are things?' you didn't tell her the latest social frivolities – you gave her a quick run-down on your caseload.

By the time the task force reported, Niav had moved on and was replaced by Ciarán Roche, who had recently come home from working in England. Ciarán turned out to be an innovator who was not afraid to push boundaries or challenge authority. On the day of its publication, Ciarán took a fiver from his pocket, telling one of the social workers to go to the Government Stationary Office and get as many copies of the Task Force Report as the money could buy. As it transpired, they were £6 each.

For weeks we studied the report. It introduced the principle of minimum intervention, whereby efforts should be directed, in the first instance, to enabling children to grow up in their own family. And it spoke of children's rights – a radical concept at a time when the Constitution protected the inalienable rights of parents over their children, and when only the marital family was considered to be the rightful and primary unit of society. In practice, this meant that we now had to drive the ambulance up from the bottom of the cliff back to the road leading to the precipice. Children still needed to be protected, but more emphasis should now be placed on joining forces with local community initiatives to better the lives of children as a whole.

*

We already had links to the community. Killarney Street had a cavernous empty hall in its centre which originally served as a waiting area. Huddled into one office to the front of it

Hanged If You Do...

were most of the social workers, spread out on a square of desks, competing for the use of two telephones. On the far side of the hall was a warren of small offices where the community workers congregated. They had a telephone of their own which, I suspected, was a hotline to the Kremlin. Those of us engaged in child protection were considered, by the community workers, as the middle-class career social workers. We in turn, considered the community workers to be leftist anti-establishment agitators. We were both right.

Tony Gregory was a regular visitor to the community workers. He was elected to Dublin City Council in 1979 but continued to teach full-time in Coláiste Eoin in Stillorgan. Unknown to the local administrator, Liz, our receptionist, took his messages and Tony would drop in for them each day after school. In Tony's first Dáil election campaign in 1981 we put up posters of him in the reception area. This was a step too far for the area administrator, who took them down, chastising us for our political partiality. I campaigned for Gregory that year. Elated with righteous idealism, I dropped in to his house one evening to declare my allegiance. In typical grumpy Gregory fashion he ran me, directing me instead to the office on Summerhill and not to be bothering him. He polled well but wasn't elected.

Drifting like a spectre between the child protection social workers and the community workers was George – a small, softly spoken Church of Ireland gentleman with an interest in choral music. Older than the rest of us, around fifty, George was the social worker that time forgot. Dating back to the very first days of health boards, when social workers did a bit of everything, George continued to work with the older people in the community. And successive supervisors just let him at it, even though the rest of us were, by then, fully occupied with children's services. George was always acquiring items of old furniture for his clients, which he stored in one of the back rooms beside the community workers. While some of us would be arguing intently at a case conference about the needs of a vulnerable child, George could be heard clattering and banging as he single-handedly lugged a wardrobe out the front door and onto the roof of his little car.

*

In response to the call of the task force for the repositioning of services from a punitive approach to a rehabilitative one, Ciarán Roche joined forces with the Daughters of Charity. Their convent on North William Street originally incorporated an orphanage. Then, moving with the times, they replaced the orphanage with a small-scale children's home in a section within the same building. More recently, the Daughters opened a family centre there as the latest iteration in their evolving ministry. The idea was that vulnerable families could attend for remedial work, such as family therapy, individual counselling and parenting skills classes, which could be undertaken in a non-threatening and safe environment. Under the old regime the message to parents was, 'You're a bad parent and if you don't get better we'll take your kids off you.' Now the message was, 'We see you have some problems – we'd like to help.' This was family support.

Family therapy became a fashionable choice on the menu of services within the new family centres. I was interviewing for staff with the Daughters of Charity at a time when the highlight of the curriculum vitae was family therapy. We ended up having to suppress a fit of the giggles every time an interviewee raised an eyebrow, lowered their tone, and announced that, you know, they were qualified in family therapy. But it was actually a valuable tool and hard work for the therapist. Once a colleague staggered out of a particularly tense and raw session with a family, only to have the mother ask him, 'Are you going back to work now?'

This was the start of a twin-track approach where we tried to straddle welfare and protection at the same time. It was often a painful contortion. Throughout the 1980s, the parameters of what constituted abuse continued to expand. Having started out with a sharp focus on physical abuse, now neglect, sexual and emotional abuse began to emerge. The so-called

12   *Hanged If You Do...*

'Kilkenny Report' was the first in a series of non-statutory inquiries into child protection matters which issued over the next two decades. An inquiry was initiated by the Department of Health after an incest case was prosecuted in the criminal court, in which shortcomings in the child protection system were revealed. The Kilkenny Incest Investigation Report (1993) not only highlighted shortcomings in the child care system, it also exposed professional ambivalence towards domestic violence and the necessity to share information across professions. It was a direct challenge to a lingering laissez-faire attitude, backed up by the Constitution, which supported the belief that what happens in the family stays in the family.

Kilkenny was the catalyst for the introduction of the long-awaited Child Care Act 1991, replacing the hopelessly outdated British Children Act 1908. The new Act placed an unequivocal responsibility on health boards to provide statutory child protection, and health boards smartly passed that responsibility onto social workers. Legislation now required responders to not only react to cases of child abuse that were brought to their attention, but to take proactive measures to identify children who are not receiving adequate care and protection. While lip service continued to be paid to welfare work, the new law provided a convenient funnel into which all child protection concerns could be poured. And they were, in large numbers, by schools, the Gardaí, voluntary organisations and others. The trajectory of child protection referrals was set irreversibly skyward.

With continued Government investment being made following the commencement of the Child Care Act, in 1995 myself and a colleague, Brid Clarke, were appointed co-directors of Child Care and Family Support Services in the Eastern Health Board. This was the first initiative in the country to provide strategic management and leadership. But in reality, we were quickly perceived as 'super social workers' by the social work teams in Dublin, Wicklow and Kildare, who referred all their unresolved problems to us. Typically, if a care placement could not be found for a child we got the five o'clock call. And if a judge wanted a scalp, or the media needed a fresh lamb to slaughter, we were it. All those crisis calls turned us into more of a management help desk than strategists for change.

Despite the reactive pressures, we managed to pull off a few policy and strategic achievements. As more money was pumped into child care services, we employed more social workers in the area of child protection. It quickly became apparent that what you get when you take on more child protection social workers is more child protection referrals. Rather than diminishing the problem it increased the volume of cases. The old adage was right in saying for every complex problem there is a simple solution that is wrong. The solution was more complex than just increasing social work numbers, which had the effect of parking the ambulance at the bottom of the cliff. The child protection element of the service needed to be balanced against more preventative services that stopped cases reaching a threshold that required protective measures. We were back to what the *Report of the Task Force on Child Care Services* had advocated in 1980.

In 1997, the Eastern Health Board undertook a review of its child care services in partnership with the trade union IMPACT, which represented social workers. Dr Norman Tutt, an English management consultant, was engaged to assist us with the task. He was a flamboyant operator who added his considerable academic and management expertise to the task. Ironically, one of his publications, *Care or Custody*, is cited in the task force report. His analysis clearly demonstrated a lack of investment in family support services and too much emphasis on child protection as a single solution. In the following years, greater investment was made in early intervention and family support by beefing up local family centres, family resource centres, neighbourhood youth projects, family support workers, community-based childcare workers and pre-school services.

But the child protection tide was still coming in. In 1999, the Department of Health and Children issued new procedures called *Children First: National Guidelines for the Protection and Welfare of Children*. It was the first time the word 'welfare' found its way into Government guidance. It also stressed the importance of early intervention and even had a chapter on family support. But, make no mistake, the primary focus was on child protection – reporting abuse, exchanging information, joint working, assessment and management.

Into the new millennium a trend emerged, whereby more referrals were being categorised as welfare rather than abuse. However, these received short shrift at the point of intake, with most being closed down straight away or soon after. There was an incompatibility between what people thought social workers did and what they actually did.

In 2006, I wrote a book called *Managing Child Welfare and Protection Services*. For the front cover I chose an image of a manager walking a tightrope. On the one hand, you had national policy telling you to take a 'whole child' approach which promoted social well-being, while on the other, you had a public expectation that no child protection case would ever be missed. And despite all the rhetoric, family support remained a spectre, devoid of the substance of well-developed theory, unlike the flesh and bones that could be broken by child abuse.

Then in 2007, I got the chance to go to a conference in Long Beach, California, to explore the Differential Response Model (DRM), an innovative approach to combining child welfare and protection. It was hosted by American Human, an organisation which has the dubious distinction of simultaneously promoting the well-being of animals as well as children. Its mission is to promote a society where no child, or animal, will ever be the victim of wilful abuse or neglect. As I write, their website homepage features a cute, if rather forlorn, mongrel with a metal dish in its mouth – a canine incarnation of Oliver Twist. On the Irish end, our trip was funded by the Children's Acts Advisory Board (CAAB), an independent State body to advise relevant Government ministers on the coordination and effective delivery of services relevant to children's legislation. Just before the country went bust, we flew business class to California, to the envy and annoyance of colleagues whose car mileages rates had just been cut. The rule of thumb in CAAB was that any flight over six hours, where you had to hit the ground running on arrival, warranted the extra leg room. Soon after our return home the agency was culled, not because of us, but because of the Government's cost-saving scrapping of State quangos in those hard times.

In any event, the State got its money's worth because we brought home the seeds of an idea that eventually grew in Ireland. Here I will take some credit, along with Dr Helen Buckley in the School of Social Work and Social Policy in Trinity College Dublin, for watering the concept of DRM at team meetings, seminars and conferences until green shoots appeared. DRM moves intervention away from a forensic-style intervention to one which remains focused on child safety, but also takes a strengths-based approach to the family as a whole. As they put itn in the USA, it moves away from the 'gotcha' mentality. It also relies heavily on the voluntary and community sectors and encourages those services to go the extra mile with families, even when there may be risks. One of the visual images I used in presentations was a move from 'hot potato', where a non-statutory service dumps their risky cases onto social work, to 'passing the baton' in a relay, requiring a synchronised and phased approach.

These elements now feature in a national model developed by the Child and Family Agency (Tusla). Established in 2014, Tusla is the new State body for child welfare and protection. The Prevention Partnership and Family Support Programme aims to embed prevention and early intervention into the culture and practice of the new agency. In essence, it seeks to intervene earlier with families who are experiencing difficulties, thus diverting them from the child protection services. Early research shows some success in dealing with families sooner rather than later. But as yet, it cannot be said that such intervention reduces the demand for child protection services. Such is that demand that at any given time there is a waiting list of high-priority child protection cases. In effect, the Agency is fishing in two entirely separate pools – prevention and protection. And the catch from the prevention pool has no appreciable effect on reducing the stock in the protection pool.

Hanged If You Do...

In the early days I worked with a clinical psychologist, Patricia Redlich. She went on to become, of all things, an agony aunt with the *Sunday Independent* until her untimely death in 2011. Anyway, way back when, Patricia summed it up perfectly when she said, 'Everybody wants to do therapy, but nobody wants the shit end of the stick.' Family support is nice, but it still falls to statutory social workers to get a dirty job done.

As it is now over thirty years since the *Report of the Task Force on Child Care Services* was published, State papers can be accessed to reveal Government thinking at the time. A memo prepared for Cabinet described the task force report as proposing an elaborate bureaucratic structure to look after what is essentially a family problem. Dr Michael Woods, Minister for Health, was at pains to point out that publication of the Government-initiated report, which took six years to prepare, should not be taken as a commitment to actually implement its recommendations. Just like the Guinness Light slogan, 'They said it couldn't be done'.

3

'Unmarried Mothers'

*I*rish folklore and social history abound with stories and report of hidden pregnancies, foundlings, infanticide and forced emigration. It is not so long ago that so-called 'unmarried mothers' and their 'illegitimate' children were both classified as social outcasts. An indelible stain remained on the character of the mother, the status of her child and the social standing of the extended family. Against such a prevailing social attitude, the only way out for a desperate woman who found herself pregnant and unmarried was to give the baby up and then to return to her old life as if nothing had ever happened. The cornerstone of a successful adoption, therefore, was secrecy.

At the foundation of the State in 1922, the non-marital birth rate was running at 2.6 per cent of all births, compared with nearly 40 per cent today. This tiny minority of 'fallen women' required moral rescue and societies, such as the Catholic Protection and Rescue Society, were established specifically for that purpose. There was a complete absence of State support, making it virtually impossible for an unmarried mother to keep her child and live independently outside an institutional setting. By the 1930s, the residential options for unmarried mothers included the original county homes; mother and baby homes, which began to emerge as a more customised

Hanged If You Do...

alternative; and private nursing homes for those who could afford them. The mother and baby homes offered refuge to the women before the birth and the means to return to the life of a maiden afterwards. This required the disposal of the baby to married couples of an appropriate faith who were deemed as deserving by the societies engaged in this work. Little consideration was given to how the mother felt about it. That wasn't the point. The objective was to return her to society with her reputation intact and to find a good home for the baby.

Prior to the introduction of adoption legislation in 1952, arrangements were made to permanently transfer the children of unmarried mothers to married couples on an ad-hoc basis. Organisations such as the Catholic Protection and Rescue Society and St Patrick's Guild arranged for the boarding out of children with suitable families. Closely aligned to the principle of secrecy was the issue of consent. Typically a 'surrender form' was signed by the mother, relinquishing all rights over the child from the moment she signed her name to it. Despite the fact that it required two people of the opposite sex to effect a pregnancy, all the responsibility was placed on the woman, with little or no inquiries being made of the man.

The Adoption Act 1952 provided for the copper-fastening of all the previous ad-hoc arrangements. The legislation also provided for the establishment of an Adoption Board to oversee and regulate adoption. The new Board introduced a consent form to be signed and sworn by the natural mother. But the system still had little insight into or regard for the mother's circumstances. No legal advice or counselling was offered to her. It is not surprising, therefore, that I have come across mothers from that era who, when seeking information years later, recognise their signature on the consent form but have no recollection of ever having signed it. Many describe parental pressure as a huge factor. But so too was the persuasion of the nuns and the adoption societies to give up the baby. Research now supports the mothers' experience that few considered they had any real choice, and most were so traumatised that the whole ordeal was a blur.

By the early 1970s, there was a softening of attitude towards unmarried mothers. This was facilitated by the Irish Women's Liberation Movement, which advocated for advisory services and legislative change, and by the establishment of Cherish, an organisation to empower these women to have a voice.

The introduction of the Unmarried Mother's Allowance in 1973 was a major enabler for women to keep their children. A steady uptake in the number of mothers and children benefiting from the allowance, corresponded with a steady decline in the number of adoptions being made. Other advances included further amendments to adoption legislation which went a long way towards ensuring that a woman's consent, when given, was fully informed.

*

Yet, even into the late 1980s, an unplanned pregnancy for a single woman could still be a crisis of catastrophic proportions. As a citizen as well as a social worker, I was shocked to hear of the death of Ann Lovett in 1984. She was a fifteen-year-old schoolgirl who died alone with her baby, having secretly given birth on church grounds at a grotto to the Virgin Mary. The perceived scandal of unmarried motherhood remained of such proportions that many women still resorted to the mother and baby homes as a means of concealing their pregnancy and secretly giving up the baby. That is why I found myself for the first time in St Patrick's Mother and Baby Home on the Navan Road, Dublin.

Word came from on high that I had to go to the placement committee which met in St Patrick's. It was the forum where children were matched with suitable families for fostering or adoption. The gravity and importance of this task was demonstrated by the fact that one of the most senior administrators in the Eastern Health Board, John Doyle, chaired the committee. Another senior administrator, Aubrey O'Brien, was also a member. He was fiercely loyal to John and vice versa. They were virtually inseparable, professionally and socially, so that, like Mary's little lamb, everywhere that John Doyle went Aubrey was sure to go. Other members of the committee comprised senior social workers and seasoned practitioners. For a novice like me, this forum was the fountain from which all knowledge and authority emanated, and the prospect of going there came between me and a good night' s sleep.

As I drove into St Patrick's for the first time the sombre, red-bricked facade frowned down at me. There were verandas on some of the four levels, like those fever hospitals where fresh air was an intrinsic part of the regime. I was directed to a solitary, squeaking chair in a dim hallway outside the parlour door. Behind it, surrounding a huge mahogany table, sat the child care elite who would summon me when they were ready to see me. At once I was back in school, outside the principal's office, waiting in guilty anticipation to be judged. Eventually, the door opened and I was called in.

I had come to the placement committee to discuss a baby I had just been allocated, who had been freed up for adoption. Another social worker had obtained the mother's consent before moving on to a different job, so I had not seen the mother or baby yet. This was a healthy seven-week-old boy who was now eligible for adoption. Having given consent, the mother had just left the mother and baby home, saying her final farewell to her son. Successfully concealing her pregnancy, she gave birth among strangers and would now resume her original life as if nothing had ever happened.

After a brief discussion on the child and his circumstances, John Doyle called for the baby to be produced at the meeting. Someone was dispatched and arrived back minutes later with a nurse holding the baby in her arms. She held him out in front of her with her hand under his bottom, like a porter at an auction presenting a vase to the room. As the child was returned to the nursery, the bidding started. Files were opened and perused. People argued the pros and cons of particular applicants, and within minutes a match was made.

I left the room and went to see the baby in the nursery upstairs. It was crammed with hospital-style cots, most of them occupied by tiny infants. No mothers were evident. Nurses, with upside-down watches pinned over their breasts, presided.

There was no mistaking that this was a hospital regime. In another room there were older children. Some of them were shuffling about, others just lying vacantly on mattresses. These were the handicapped children who were left over from countless placement committee meetings, because families could not be found for them.

St Patrick's was managed by the Eastern Health Board but under the auspices of the Daughters of Charity. As well as the placement committee convening there, there was a health board social worker in the home who did most of the liaising with mothers in the weeks before and after their confinement. It was a valuable placement resource for social workers who worked with legions of unmarried mothers who still sought refuge in the mother and baby homes which were positioned around the country.

This was my first introduction to the Daughters of Charity, whom I admired because of their dedication to the most marginalised, and their commitment to high standards. That is why it grieves me now when I go online and see former residents of St Patrick's describe themselves as 'survivors'. While this language no doubt accurately describes their experience, there is another story that is not being heard just now. It is the story of how society at large used the mother and baby home system as a convenient carpet under which it could sweep its own secrets and lies.

*

Around that time, I worked with a schoolgirl who managed to conceal her pregnancy right up to the point of going into labour. She was watching television with her family one night when the contractions started. She left the living room, slipped on her coat, and left the house. Somehow she got herself as far as the porter's office in the Rotunda Hospital, where she gave birth. Such was the depth of her unconscious denial that she was almost as shocked as her parents that a baby was born.

By contrast, I worked with another pregnant woman whom we knew would never be able to care for her baby, but who never had any intention of placing her for adoption. She was a street drinker whose other children were all in care. In those days, previous history didn't count and there was no legal way to protect the baby from her without first giving her a chance. You couldn't go to court and speculate on what you thought would happen. You had to present evidence of what had actually happened. Given the mother's addiction and life-style, this posed a high risk for the infant. To offset that risk, we arranged to place mother and child in Eglington House, which was the successor of St Patrick's Mother and Baby Home. Still staffed by the Daughters of Charity, it was a progressive service which tolerated behaviour from mothers that other services would not. As we expected and (to be honest) hoped, this mother disappeared without her child after a few nights. The baby was made subject of a court order and remained in foster care for the duration of her childhood.

As I write the Mother and Baby Home Commission has just completed its long inquisition into how these single women entered these institutions, the extent of the mothers' partic-ipation in decision-making, the living arrangements and care arrangements, mortality rates and post-mortem practices. Its publication has refuelled public outrage at what went on behind closed doors .

I was in the room when Dr James Reilly, Minister for Children and Youth Affairs, launched the work of the Commission. A lot of hurt and wounded people had gathered there and you could hear the emotion in the Minister's own voice in response to them. But it doesn't take a soothsayer to predict that the hurt will remain, even now that the Commission has expended its €25 million and apportioned blame. Because hurt like that is indelible, like the shame that drove the young women to seek refuge in the first place. However, in the rush to judgement, we must remember that the nuns who ran the mother and baby homes did not go out and procure those young women. They were brought to them by their families, and by stalwarts of the community such as priests and general practitioners. The mother and baby home was the receptacle for those vulnerable young women who were banished by their communities in the first place.

It would be nice to think that all that was behind us and that we have all moved on. Yet in 2016 the body of a dead infant was found at a recycling plant in County Wicklow. And in 2018, in the week before Christmas, a newborn baby's body was found partially buried on a beach in Balbriggan, Co. Dublin. What desperation, what ostracisation, can still lead a young mother to risk not only her baby's life but her own in a final effort to keep a nativity secret?

4

The Gorman

*I*n the 163 years between its establishment and my first visit to it, little had been done to soften the fact that this institution was anything other than an asylum. The Richmond Lunatic Asylum first opened in 1815 in Grange-gorman, Dublin, as a national repository for fools and the mad. It was later rebranded as St Brendan's Psychiatric Hospital but the colloquial name of 'The Gorman' still stuck. The original high walls were replaced by railings, and many of the original austere stone buildings lay derelict. But plenty too were still in use, protruding from the grassy estate like a vast set for a Halloween extravaganza. Although the permanently open front gates were an invitation into the fifty-five acres of inner-city greenery, it was not a place where local residents chose to walk the dog.

This was 1978 and I had just started as a social worker in the psychiatric service. I arrived straight from a long student placement in Purdysburn Psychiatric Hospital on the outskirts of Belfast. That was an old hospital too, but the original buildings were converted into posh modern offices, and new bungalow-style units were built for the patients around the grounds. For this reason, it required the dexterity of a time traveller for me to make the necessary adjustment from one hospital regime to the other.

But things were looking up. Ivor Browne was the chief psychiatrist and he had just produced a plan setting out the vision for the delivery of mental health services into the future. It centred on the scaling down of the large mental hospitals and the development of comprehensive community-based services in the form of day hospitals, day centres and outpatient clinics. Browne was also Professor of Psychiatry in UCD. He was a brave choice for both posts because of his radical approach to theory and practice. He advocated against the overuse of medication, particularly for depression. He favoured talking therapies in an era which still widely practiced electroshock therapy, as well as drug therapy. Lobotomy had been phased out as a means of permanent patient control. This had entailed drilling holes into a patient's forehead and jiggling the frontal lopes with an implement that resembled a knitting needle. These patients could still be seen shuffling aimlessly around the hospital grounds. They were easily recognisable by the tell-tale circular scars on their foreheads, as if demonic horns had been removed. Wearing other people's clothes from a communal wardrobe, they looked like adult-sized orphans as they pottered about in a permanent state of mindless subjugation.

Ivor Browne was Ireland's answer to R.D. Laing, the Scottish psychiatrist who attained pop star status – much like Christiaan Barnard had achieved for his work on human heart transplantation in the 1960s. Laing's theory was that patient feelings should not be restrained by chemical or electronic interventions. Like Ken Keasey, in *The Electric Kool-Aid Acid Test*, who advocated the benefits of the psychedelic experience brought on by LSD, Browne was open to radical new ideas. And the more they challenged the establishment, the better. He was the go-to person for the media, and he seemed to like that. At one stage we had offices close to each other in St Brendan's. After moments of stress or frustration you could hear Ivor marching briskly down to the toilets at the top of the stairs with his tin whistle. There, using the cubical as his studio, he whistled while he worked.

*

I ducked through the gothic arch doorway and looked up at the huge, large stone steps leading to a heavy wooden door, like a boy at the bottom of a beanstalk. I climbed up the dim stairway and faced it. There was no intercom or bell. The centre panel was faded and scraped from generations of hands banging upon it. I added mine, first with my knuckles, then pounding with the side of my fist. No one came. A huge keyhole eyed me suspiciously. It must have needed a turnkey the size of a jack handle to unlock the door.

I tapped with my car keys. The door creaked open, Hitch-cock-style. An enormous female nurse peered around it, brandishing a key as big as a poker. She was surrounded by a gaggle of female patients who eyed me with the unabashed curiosity of little children. One old woman, her face half-deflated like a wrinkled balloon, pawed my shoulder as if she were petting a foal. 'Are you the doctor?', she asked over and over as she shuffled alongside me, exposing the gummy interior of her cavernous mouth. I had come to see Pauline. She wanted to see her children, who were in residential care and had been long before her admission to hospital. They were taken from her because of her chaotic lifestyle. She found it impossible to hold down a flat and often lived on the street for long periods. Her request to see her girls, and her anxiety around it, came up at a team meeting and that's where I came in. The nun in charge of the children's home was understandably reluctant to expose the children to their mother's current whereabouts, in a locked ward. Pauline was a temporary patient (a euphemism for compulsory) and, as such, was not allowed out of the ward on her own. So I suggested that I would bring her to see the girls, and this was agreed.

Before setting up the access visit, I wanted to get to know Pauline a little bit first. The nurse walked me down a long, bare corridor. Freedom beckoned through the windows on the left from which the city and the mountains beyond could be seen. On the right, there were disused cells, some with the remnants of padding on the walls. From behind other doors I could hear wailing and shouting as I glued myself to the nurse.

When I met Pauline in an open area beside the nurses' station, I realised that we had met before. She was a regular at the Simon Community night shelter, where I volunteered one evening a week before going to college to do social work. She was a street drinker. Once she was allocated a Corporation flat, but she blew up her kitchen trying to light the gas oven with a cigarette. Pauline had three daughters and was genuinely excited about the prospect of seeing them in the children's home. It had been a long time. Then there was the added bonus of temporary release from the locked ward, which she saw as a vote of trust in her progress.

On the day of the visit I arrived in my Renault 4. She was ready and waiting – all dolled up, but her lipstick and makeup looked like it had been applied in the dark. Her black hair was cut short. She wore a black skirt that was too small for her after so many institutional dinners, and a black leatherette jacket over a white blouse. She quaked with nervousness as we got ready to go. She wanted to get sweets or something for the girls so she had negotiated the release of some of her funds, which were under staff control.

The children's home, like so many, was in the corner of convent grounds where an orphanage once stood. This was a modern, detached house, big like a doctor's house at the end of a suburban street. Children's homes were largely the domain of female religious orders, having evolved from the old orphanages which the nuns previously ran. Typically, these homes had no more than nine child residents, minded by a roster of residential staff, and always with a nun in charge.

We were greeted at the door of the home by the manager, a small, frail and timid nun. In full habit and veil, her head was missing except the face, which protruded like a mask at a masquerade ball. Whispering a breathless welcome to Pauline, it was a toss-up as to which of them was the more nervous. When the nun shook my hand, hers felt like chicken bones wrapped in clingfilm. We were ushered into the parlour just inside the hall door and the girls were sent for. They arrived, shy and uncertain, in their Sunday best. By now Pauline was a relative stranger to them. They lined up in single file to kiss the makeup that was plastered to her cheek.

Jenny and Sheila were thirteen-year-old twins, and little Sarah was just ten. For a while we sat there in the parlour, manufacturing conversation out of the silence. I was partially submerged in a sofa, buoyed up by floral cushions. The nun, whom all the children in the home called Mother, served tea in dainty china cups. We ate apple tart and chocolate biscuits from plates that matched the cups. The sipping and nibbling was amplified in the self-conscious silence.

After an hour or so we began to move out of the confines of the parlour. The girls showed their mother their rooms, and she met some of the other children. Pauline asked if it was okay to bring Sarah across the road to a shop to buy her some sweets. I agreed as I continued to chat with the twins.

We were all more at ease now, and I was beginning to think of heading back to the hospital. Pauline went upstairs to the bathroom. She was gone a long time and I hoped the prospect of separating from the girls wasn't upsetting her. When she came back she was more relaxed. She quipped that I must be in my element surrounded by all these women. Laughing too much at her own joke, she slapped my thigh. Then, her mood changed in an instant as she turned to the nun. In a growl that ascended in volume with every word, she said, 'And another thing, you. You're not their fucking mother!'

The nun put her hands to her chest as if she had been shot. Then her hands flapped franticly at her lap, as if the words could be brushed away like crumbs from the apple tart. Suppressing a flash of panic, I realised Pauline was drunk. There was an off-licence beside the sweet shop across the road. Using Sarah as a decoy, she had bought her stash and downed it in the bathroom when she got back.

Mother jumped up and ushered the girls out of the room. They left in tears as the other children gathered around the doorway with a collective expression that registered somewhere between horror and amusement.

Eventually, somehow, I got Pauline into the car and away from there. She ranted on about being locked up in the hospital.

Then she announced that she wasn't going back. I threatened that she would be in deep trouble if she didn't go back and that all her privileges would be taken away. That made her laugh. At the same time, I was thinking she might not be the only one to face the music after this mess.

'Just drop me off in town. Please,' she pleaded like a little kid. But then she switched tack. She placed her hand on my knee and in a husky whisper repeated, 'Please'. With one hand on the wheel, I fended her off with the other.

Then she got nasty. 'Well fuck off then,' she barked, opening the door as the car was still moving. She struggled with the seat belt but couldn't undo it. So she took off one of her shoes and started to beat me around the head with it. By then we were in College Green in a line of traffic which was stopped at a red light. I put my arms over my head to protect myself as she really started to clatter me. Then, through my arms, I saw a garda car just ahead of us. I flashed the lights. At first there was no response, but after a few more attempts two gardaí got out of their car and came back to us.

I explained as coherently as possible that I was a social worker in charge of a patient from a secure ward in a psychiatric hospital, who had got drunk in my care and, having failed to seduce me, was now assaulting me. One of the gardaí looked the car up and down as if trying to spot a hidden camera. 'Is this a wind-up?' he smiled. But Pauline became even more agitated at the sight of the gardaí. 'Pigs', she shouted, as she beat me some more with her shoe before throwing it at the garda. She tugged violently at her seatbelt.

The gardaí explained that they were not in their jurisdiction and were returning down the country having escorted money to Dublin. But they could see that she was causing a breach of the peace, so they cuffed her and stuffed her into the back of the patrol car. With their blue light flashing and Pauline bouncing around in the back seat, they drove to Pearse Street Garda station with me following behind in my Renault 4.

She was put into a cell. The two arresting gardaí headed off as I sat in reception wondering what next. Eventually, a desk sergeant called me in behind the counter. 'What's your rela-tionship to this woman?' he snapped.

'I'm not a relative', I explained, repeating the account I had given the other gardaí at College Green.

'Well, you needn't think you'll be getting another garda escort to bring that woman back to hospital. We have real police work to do you know.'

Begrudgingly, he allowed me to use the phone and I even-tually managed to organise an ambulance to take Pauline back to the hospital. As she was being frog-marched from the cell by two male nurses, the sergeant turned to me and asked, 'What sort of a hospital would let a woman as mad as that out with an amateur like you?'

'It's not a hospital', I assured him 'It's an asylum.'

5

Rat Trap

I used to do an outpatient clinic with the psychiatric services in the North Strand Health Centre, just beside the Five Lamps. The Lamps are a well-known landmark at the intersection of five streets, comprising five ornamental lanterns with drinking fountains below. They were erected in the 1880s with money bequeathed by Lieutenant General Henry Hall, a Galway man who ended up in the Bengal Army. After an adventurous life he died in his bed back in Ireland. Being an advocate of temperance, he willed the money to promote sobriety. His aspirations went astray however, because for years some of the lamps directly faced public houses and now the Five Lamps is the name of a brewery. In the 1980s, 100 years after its erection, the site became better known as 'Handbag Corner', because it was a notorious junction for smash-and-grabs as cars pulled up at the various sets of traffic lights. Handbags left on the passenger seat were the favourite target of youngsters who smashed the passenger window with a hammer, terrorising the driver and then helping themselves. The location even got a mention in the Boomtown Rats' big hit, 'Rat Trap': 'Just down past the gasworks, by the meat factory door/The Five Lamp boys were coming on strong...'.

The fountains on the Five Lamps provided fresh water to locals who had no running water in their homes. But even into

the 1980s many of the surrounding flats had no bathroom facilities despite some of their grandiose names, such as St Joseph's
Mansions. This, combined with the tenements which were
still occupied around Summerhill and Seán McDermott Street,
created a latter-day *Strumpet City*. The adjacent docklands
had been a traditional source of employment in the north inner
city; but with the introduction of containers and mechanisa-
tion this valuable work stream was lost, adding to the overall
depression of the locality. In 1978, Dublin Corporation came
up with a development plan which included the demolition of
the tenements. But the problem was, there was no guarantee
that families would be rehoused in the same locality. As it transpired, hundreds of families were displaced under the scheme.

One older couple I knew were rehoused with some of their
children and grandchildren from Seán McDermott Street to a
new house around the corner, off Summerhill Parade. Far from
enjoying the modern advantages of their new home, they were
bereft, pining like refugees for the old neighbourhood. They
continued to attend Mass at Laurence O'Toole Church in Seán
McDermott Street, and their fervent wish was to be buried out
of it.

My frosted upstairs window in the health centre gave me
an opaque overview of all this. On many mornings I even saw
Charlie Haughey passing the Five Lamps in the back of his State
car on the way to work as Taoiseach. I never met him but I came
close once. As Minister for Health, he opened a new wing of St
Vincent's Psychiatric Hospital in Fairview. I was in a line of staff
on the drive outside, assembled to greet him on arrival. He got
out of the car and started walking down the line shaking hands.
When he was about three people away a seagull, obviously a
Tony Gregory supporter, crapped on me, splattering my jacket,
shirt and hair. I stepped out of line and went inside to clean
up. Back inside Archbishop Dermot Ryan did a blessing before
the Minister was asked to speak. When Haughey took to the
platform he had to bring the mic stand down a few notches.
'And they say I don't look up to the clergy,' he said. As Minister
for Health Haughey introduced the 1979 Family Planning Bill
legalising contraception, albeit in a very restrictive way. The

purchase of a packet of condoms required a medical prescription to be dispensed by a pharmacist. Implicitly too, it was limited to married couples. It was a mixed source of hilarity and irritation to the psychiatrists in the North Strand clinic.

The clinic was held upstairs in the health centre, beside the dental clinic. On busy days the two queues converged as the patients for both services waited on plastic bucket chairs. This usually resulted in chair wars between both services as staff from each tugged disputed property from each other. The matter was finally settled when the word 'Dental' was daubed onto the back of a row of chairs in Tipex.

The two regular consultant psychiatrists would see the patients first, assess their progress, adjust their meds and then pass a selection of them on to me for a longer session. Anyone with young children would automatically come into me. They waited silently, the occupant of each chair a chapter in the biography of wounded lives which the clinicians and I wrote each week.

*

Mary was a regular. She had several children. Her parenting skills were fine and she always had them well turned out. But she was very anxious, about everything. It was hard to keep her focused on any one area at time. She took up too much time at outpatients, particularly with a line waiting, so I arranged to see her once a week outside the clinic hours.

Every week I did a home visit while the children were at school, trying to confine the session to an hour. I drew the anxiety out of her like a poultice, but it always seemed to end up in me afterwards. She was always smartly dressed for these sessions, like she was going out for the night. The good cups came out and not so much as a piece of Lego revealed that children ever lived there.

During one of these sessions her husband came home. I hadn't met him before, but from Mary's accounts I knew he roughed her up a bit. He had on a 'what's all this' expression. I wasn't sure if he knew she attended the psychiatric clinic. He joked that he came home unexpectedly only to find me with his wife. We finished up and Mary started to tidy up, brining cups into the kitchen. He followed her. I could hear harsh whispering as I got up to leave. As I headed for the door he stood in front of me to open it. We were nose to nose. I could smell beer, but he could smell fear.

A few days later he called to the office. Bypassing reception, he wandered around until he found me. He was drunk. Prodding my chest with a rigid, hairy finger he told me Mary wouldn't be going back to outpatients. And if he ever saw me around his fucking gaff again he'd fucking do me. Fair enough, but he didn't leave it there. For weeks he called around on pay day. He was always so drunk that he was tongue-tied. But each time it was the same in-your-face, spit-splashing threats.

The threats worked because I started to make myself scarce on his pay days. But my timing was off because once I met him coming in the door as I was walking out. I kept going but he followed me. The car was parked on the roadside just outside, so I hopped in and locked the door. I so wanted to give him the finger from the safety of my cocoon. He tried the door and when he couldn't open it he stood back and, summoning noxious bile from the depts of his nicotine-encrusted lungs, spat on the window. A glutinous blob of emerald phlegm slid drunkenly down the pane. Then he kicked the driver door a few times with the sole of his foot, staggering as he balanced on one leg.

I've been thumped and hand-bagged plenty of times. It's easy to take it from someone who lashes out in a moment of high tension or exasperation. But what got me with this guy was the menacing uncertainty – the not being sure if, or exactly when, he was going to show up and get physical. Now I really knew what his wife was going through. I was experiencing a real-time enactment of domestic violence.

This was at a time when little was done by social services to assist women trapped in such situations, and the Gardaí were seldom interested in intervening. I once persuaded a woman to press charges, walking her to the Garda station to make a statement. When it came to court her husband didn't show up

- but neither did she. 'Told you', the garda said to me as the case was dismissed.

*

Kevin was another regular to the clinic. As tough guys go, Mary's husband was a Hare Krishna compared to him. But Kevin liked me, and that was the difference. He was very tall and built like a heavyweight fighter. The scars on his face and limbs catalogued all the confrontations that had one thing in common – he never backed down. Kevin was never going to play the role of the docile outpatient waiting in line on a bucket chair. He simply burst into my office each time he arrived, whether I was with someone or not, like a four-year-old asking if I was coming out to play.

Kevin spent his early childhood in the Artane Industrial School, where he had his innocence beaten out of him. This resulted in an oppositional defiant disorder where he challenged all forms of authority and needed to impose himself on others, through brute force if necessary. His attitude got him into a lot of trouble. He prided himself in the amount of pain he could withstand. He had a gladiatorial attitude to combat – death or glory. He drank too much and his fatalistic attitude let him to try any mood-altering compound without fear. When I queried this with him, he said, 'Fuck tomorrow,' which pretty much summed up his fatalistic take on life. But there is a thin line between fatalism and hopelessness, where despair often masquerades as bravado.

Kevin liked talking to me and would sometimes unwittingly expose a real vulnerability. Once he described walking into the psychiatric clinic as like walking into a convent. He valued the atmosphere of calm, which afforded him some fleeting monastic contemplation. He had been living in hotels since his last spell in prison and was looking for a small flat to keep him off the streets. Despite his lifestyle, he always looked sharp and could easily pass himself off as a reasonable tenant to a landlord. But our efforts were thwarted when Kevin got himself locked up after thrashing a fastfood restaurant in a row over portion sizes.

I went to see him in Mountjoy. I climbed through a little wooden gate cut into the massive main gate, as if I were arriving from Lilliput. The officer who let me in was massive and ungainly, with a neck as thick as a telegraph pole. A small, peaked cap teetered on his enormous bald head, like Humpty Dumpty.

Kevin had already been confined to the basement because they always found him too hard to manage in the main prison. Even in the maximum security of the basement he rattled the cage. He could do solitary confinement and bread and water, no problem. He expected it. But his golden ticket was self-harming.

Like a number of hardened prisoners, Kevin knew that the one thing the screws could not ignore was his health. And the one way to get out of the basement, out of the prison itself, was to do something to himself. So he swallowed anything he could find – bits of cutlery or parts of his bed – or he would cut himself with any rough edge he could find. Once he embedded a spring from his bed into his abdomen like a corkscrew. Most of these episodes landed him in hospital, but that was the plan. From the prison authority's perspective, all he was doing was extended his imprisonment by getting add-ons for bad behaviour. But, as he saw it, he was thwarting the system by never relinquishing control of his own destiny.

The big prison officer escorted me to the basement. A single spiral stairway was the only way in and the only way out. On a wall by the door an inmate had scraped, 'So and so was here – and may return.' The whole centre space was empty like a church without pews. It was damp, dark and musty. The cells lined the walls, which were being patrolled by cockroaches. Each cell door had a little grill at eye level. I could feel all the eyes sizing me up, as I made a mental list of their infamous owners. Suddenly I felt a tap on my shoulder from behind. My feet left the ground. Kevin, chained by the wrist to two prison officers, laughed out loud at my feebleness.

When he got out he came to see me often. But always on his terms – when he liked. He would become petulant like a toddler if I wasn't there, or ready to see him straight away. He was using a lot of heroin. Once he was shooting up at the sink in the bathroom of a fastfood restaurant when a couple of customers came in. 'What the fuck are you looking at?' he barked, and they were gone. He hadn't even bothered to seek out any semblance of privacy.

Then he went into a cubical where he hacked at the inside of his forearms with a Stanley knife. A nurse in the A&E Department in Jervis Street Hospital telephoned me to let me know. I got on to the social worker in the Drug Treatment Centre in Jervis Street, seeking to have him admitted. She was unmoved:

'Why should we take him in?' she asked.

'Because he tried to kill himself.'

'But he didn't,' she countered.

I argued that he wouldn't need a bed if he was dead. But I was told that I should not enable such attention-seeking behaviour, and that was the end of it. He spent a few days on an acute ward and was discharged with his arms wrapped up like a mummy.

A few months later Kevin got a flat in a different part of town. His visits became less frequent and eventually we lost touch. A couple of years later I got a call from the social worker in Jervis Street to say that he had died. He had contracted a liver disease through intravenous drug use. Kevin, the warrior, did not die in glorious battle. He died slowly and alone in his bed.

At his funeral I recognised some of the prison officers, sheepishly loitering outside the church, hands in their pockets, as the coffin was loaded into the hearse. The big one came over to me. He said, 'He was his own worst enemy, you know.'

'I do', is all I could say.

As I drove back to the office I turned on the car radio. The Boomtown Rats were singing his epitaph: 'It's a rat trap – and you've been caught.'

6

'Am I Going to Heaven?'

*I*t was dark before we got out of court and it was raining hard. By the time I got back to the car my trousers were stuck to my legs. I prayed the car would start. Why do emergencies always happen in bad weather? I was with another social worker who came along to give me a hand. I had just given evidence that a child was at immediate risk. The judge granted a place of safety order. It's like a search warrant, except the thing to be retrieved is a child. The order was made on my sworn evidence alone. There had to be a compelling and urgent reason for a judge to grant such an order without hearing evidence from the other side. There would be another day for a full hearing when solicitors for the health board and the parent would unpack their evidence with arguments before the court. But right now we had to go and find the child.

The thing about emergency care orders is that is that there is no time to prepare the child for what is going to happen. You need the element of surprise, otherwise you run the risk of the parents absconding with the child.

Joan was a patient in the psychiatric service on the North Strand, where I did a weekly clinic. Mainly she was maintained at outpatients. On the odd occasion when she needed hospital-isation, her mother used to come over from England and mind her daughter, Milly, who was six. Lately though, things were not going well between Joan and her family. When I checked with social services over there they were saying her mother had her own problems and they were not supportive of her minding Milly in the future.

'Can I take it that the child has been placed on the At Risk Register?', the English social worker had asked, her imperious tone oozing with condescension. It never occurs to them that in other jurisdictions people might do things differently. When I told her we didn't have such a thing, she was aghast. 'Well, report me to the Queen then', I wanted to say.

Joan was missing outpatient appointments. When I called around to her flat she was reluctant to let me in. Her face peered through a crack in the door and she kept looking over her shoulder nervously, as if she was being followed. Her speech was rapid and saliva bubbled on the corners of her mouth. I gave her a new appointment to see the psychiatrist, which she said she would keep, but she didn't.

The following week I got a call from Milly's school. Her attendance had become patchy and when she did turn up she was looked worried and bedraggled. So I made another home visit. Joan let me in this time after a lot of cajoling. The place was a mess. I remained standing because the couch had what we called 'sticky sofa syndrome'. Clothes were draped over every chair. The kitchen area smelled like putrid meat and the sink was clogged with tea bags. Joan was still very shifty, glancing over her shoulder and speaking only in a whisper. I asked to see Milly. When she appeared from the bedroom she looked jaded and wan.

I made a deal with Joan. She had to attend outpatients and Milly had to go to school. But when I checked with the school a few days later Milly had not attended. Neither did Joan visit the psychiatrist when she was supposed to. Next day I made another home visit and this time Milly answered the door.

'Is it about Mammy?', she asked, peering through a crack in the door as her mother had done. I said it was and asked to see her.

'She's not here', Milly said.

'What do you mean? Where is she? Are you on your own in there?'

'I thought you were going to tell me where she was,' she said, opening the door to let me in.

It turned out Joan had gone out the previous evening around Milly's bedtime. She said she had things to do but that she would be back soon. Milly told me that this had never happened before, but that she wasn't scared. She had made toast for her breakfast. She said she could make loads of things but she kept away from the kettle because she wasn't allowed near it.

I gathered up a few of Milly's belongings. She took her bunny from the bed and we walked the short way to my office. I was just fixing her something to eat when I got a call from the psychiatrist at outpatients. Joan had dropped in without an appointment. She was gibberish, freezing and exhausted. It seemed she had just been wandering around by herself all night. She agreed with the doctor that she needed to be admitted and they wanted her to come in straight away. I brought Milly around to link up with her mother in the outpatients. The dressing-down for leaving Milly alone would have to wait. First, I had to find a care placement for Milly.

We made a plan that Milly and Joan would go back to their place. When I found a short-term foster home I would call around to finalise arrangements. Milly would need to be prepared for what to expect. Joan could help with this before admitting herself to hospital. Children always took it better when their parents endorsed an admission to care.

I started phoning foster homes from a long list, doing a sales job on the child. No, she is perfectly well-behaved, quiet as a mouse, doesn't wet the bed and would eat anything. There are never enough foster homes and it is a sickening feeling when you need to find one in a hurry. Eventually, after a number of anxious phone calls, I got lucky. One of my pet families said yes, with very few questions asked. I punched the air as I hung up the phone.

When I called over to Milly and Joan there was no response to my knocking. Peering through the window, there was no sign of life. Then a woman on the balcony came over. She said that

Joan had been up and down the stairs a few times with plastic bags full of clothes and things. She seemed very agitated. I hadn't anticipated it, but Joan had obviously scarpered with the child.

I high-tailed it back to the office and talked it over with the senior social worker. She reasoned that Joan had never been a physical threat to Milly. She had done some harmful things when she went off the rails, but nothing dangerous up to now. Maybe we would just have to wait it out. She told me to report the incident to the Gardaí. I went around to Mountjoy Street but I needn't have bothered. The guy at the desk had that faraway look, like the few times I reported my car radio stolen. It was an expression that said, 'You'll never see that again.'

After a restless night I went into the office first thing and called Joan's mother in England. She agreed to let me know if Milly turned up. I couldn't think of anywhere else she might go. I also phoned social services in England, putting them on alert. I made some other calls but there was no trace of the pair. After another day and night our office received a call from the landlady in a boarding house. A woman with a child had rented a room and she was becoming concerned. She holed up all day and wandering around at night. She had not heard a sound from the child since she moved in. It had to be them. A colleague whom Joan would not recognise went around to check things out. It was them alright.

So we went to court and got a place of safety order. We needed to get Milly out of there at the same time as the hospital would send a team out to intercept her mother. So we were synchronising our movements with the psychiatric nurses who were coming for Joan. It was important to have the exact name and address on the order. If Joan were to move location the order would be invalid, so it was urgent that we got a move on. These warrants were actually made out to the local garda superintendent to search for and remove a named child. In practice, the gardaí just accompanied the social workers in case there was a breach of the peace. By the time we got the order it was after office hours and dark. We headed to the garda station nearest the boarding house and presented the order to the garda at the desk. He read it carefully and then announced, 'The Super is having his tea.'

I stressed the urgency and how we needed to intercept Joan while she was still at that address. 'I just told you,' he said, 'he's having his tea.'

We sat. After half an hour or so the superintendent showed up. He looked at the order, looked at us, then back to the order. Writing something on it, he pushed it back to the garda on the desk without saying a word. Then he disappeared into his office, presumably to do something more important than rescuing a child. We continued to sit, watching every move at the reception window, ears pricked like anxious dogs waiting to go for walk. After a few minutes, three gardaí came out and invited us behind the front desk. I wanted to kiss them.

We headed for the boarding house, the gardaí in their squad car and us following behind in my car. The psychiatric nurses were already outside and an ambulance was parked a little bit down the road. We agreed that I would go in for Milly first and they would then go in for Joan when she was safely removed. We had tipped off the landlady so she was expecting us all. She let us in, gesticulating with elaborate hand signals to Joan's door, as if she were guiding a jet to a parking bay. Then she disappeared into the depths of the house.

We tiptoed up the stairs. But Joan must have seen us coming because she was standing on the landing looking down. Instead of going into the room and slamming the door she just stood there slapping herself, tugging at her clothes and wailing. The biblical reference to people in great calamity renting their garments suddenly became apparent. Her worst fears were realised – they really were coming to take her away.

When we reached the top of the stairs she ran into the room, leaving the door wide open. Sitting on the floor behind the bed, she wrapped herself around Milly. The child was crying and screaming too. She had no idea what was going on. Four grown-ups – two uniformed gardaí and two social workers – had just invaded her world.

Usually when a child is coming into care you negotiate with the parents and hopefully reach agreement that it's for the best. And it's not always forever. It can be just until a particular problem is fixed or a crisis abated. The best care plans are the ones made with the cooperation and consent of the parents. But when you are executing a place of safety order, a decision has already been taken to remove a child without parental consent or knowledge. Entering a bedroom with a warrant in your hand is not the time for negotiation. I needed to do what I came for. So I grabbed Milly while two gardaí restrained Joan.

If Plan A had worked and Joan had cooperated, we would have been able introduce the idea of being minded by another family to Milly. There would have been introductions and story books depicting the placement process. There would also have been transitional objects, such as keepsakes or a special toy, that Milly could leave in the foster home in anticipation of her placement. Now, in this crisis, the other social worker simply stuffed what things she could find, including her bunny, into a paper sack.

I carried Milly out of the room but put her down at the top of the stairs. Joan broke free from the gardaí and grabbed Milly. She made for the bathroom at the top of the landing and turned the key. We could hear banging, then the sound of broken glass.

'She's trying to get out the window', one of the gardaí said. Another ran down the stairs and out the back. The rest of us were frozen, wondering what to do next. Then the other garda retuned with a lump hammer. Where it came from, I still don't know. In two blows he was through the panel nearest the door handle. He reached in and turned the key.

Joan was crouched beside the toilet bowl with her hands on her head. Milly stood with her back to the door with her arms around her mother, shielding her. I reached in and tugged Milly by the wrist. Joan stood up and grabbed her, slapping us with her other hand. As two of the gardaí wrestled Joan I prised her arms from around Milly and made a run for the car with the child. On cue the psychiatric nurses then ran into the house.

Hanged If You Do...

In slamming the car shut, I had locked Milly out of her whole world and into a vortex of uncertainty.

*

When I was Milly's age I was abruptly admitted to a fever hospital. The ambulance came to the house, my parents kissed me goodbye and I was gone. At first, I was in an isolation ward – my parents would come and wave at me through a porthole in the door. I beckoned them to come in, but they never did. Nobody ever explained what was going on.

Later, I was transferred to a ward with other children. We would talk to each other but I still missed home. There was a light hanging from the ceiling near my bed. It hung from a stiff cable and the shade was a pearl-coloured orb, like a crystal ball. When I looked into it, I could see my friends playing on the green outside our next-door neighbour's front garden. I waved to them often, and even called out, but they never noticed me.

When I started to feel better and looked to get up, I was placed in a restraining jacket which fastened me to the bed. My parents came every week. Now they had to share a porthole with other parents. When it was their turn to wave I hid under the bed clothes until they were gone.

*

My colleague sat in the back of the car with Milly. The child was shivering and clung tightly to her. 'She'd climb into me if she could', the social worker said.

Milly was silent as we drove to the foster home. We tried to explain what was happening. Her mother would not be there. She wasn't going home. She was going somewhere else. She would be met by nice people that she didn't know. They lived in a lovely house. They had a dog.

Then Milly looked up into the social worker's face and whispered, 'Am I going to Heaven?'

The foster parents were welcoming and kind. They made Milly hot chocolate, which she drank. When it was time to go Milly became clingy and upset. Separating from a child at a time of crisis is not easy. I was the only person she knew, and I was about to leave her with strangers. I went to the car and took out a notebook and pen. I asked Milly to mind them for me overnight, but that I would be back in the morning to collect them.

The following morning when I returned, Milly was sitting at the kitchen table eating coco pops. She looked lovely and fluffy. Her bunny was sitting on the table beside her bowl. She was relaxed. We chatted, and then she said, 'When Mammy comes to see me, is it okay if I ask her can I stay here for a while?'

7

Improper Guardianship

We were operating under the old British Children Act 1908 which, like an old suit at the back of the wardrobe, had seen better days. The Act was still sporting a top hat and tails right into the 1970s and 1980s. Laws codify behaviour, but societal values change and laws have to be changed to catch up with them. It is now socially unacceptable to employ children as chimney sweeps – yet in 1908 it was a splendid solution for cleaning those crusty crevices where adults couldn't reach. In fact, legislation in Ireland governing the employment of child chimney sweeps was forgotten over time and only repealed in 2018.

In its day, the Children Act was hailed as the Children's Charter because it amounted to a bill of rights for children. Building on the work of social reformers in the mid-nineteenth century, the legislation was an overdue response to the plight of so many children who lived and worked in appalling conditions. The Act was a real recognition of society's duty to children who, having no control over their own destiny, needed the State to recognise them as dependants rather than human assets. For the first time children were given the status of protected persons.

The Act abolished the death sentence for children and set the age of criminal responsibility at seven years. Prior to the passing of the Act children over seven were considered to know the difference between right and wrong and could, in theory at least, die on the gallows like adults if found guilty of serious felonies. When I was a child I was taught that the 'age of reason' within the Catholic Church was seven years. As with the British legislation, this had the expectation that children could distinguish between venial sins, which were minor offences, and mortal sins, which were grave offences. To die with a mortal sin on your soul meant perpetual suffering in the flames of Hell. If, as a seven-year-old, I had to choose between hanging in a state of grace or living in mortal sin, I would have happily chosen execution in this life over eternal damnation in the next. In Ireland, it was 2006 before the age of criminal responsibility was raised from seven to twelve years. This higher age threshold is still low by European standards. We now have an anomaly where children cannot consent to medical treatment until they are sixteen, but they can be sentenced for criminal offences from the age of twelve.

Building on earlier legislation, the issue of cruelty to children was strengthened by the 1908 Act when parental neglect causing suffering was outlawed. The Act also prescribed for the protection of infant life, where children under seven years were being minded for reward by substitute carers, such as wet nurses. Now carers had to inform the local authority that they were minding a child. They also had to inform the coroner if a child died in their care. As a precaution against murder, the minders were prohibited from taking out insurance on children in their care. They were also made subject to visitation from inspectors who were empowered to take the child to a place of safety if necessary. These were the bones of legislation that we social workers operated under until the eventual commencement of the Child Care Act 1991. When I started in 1978, regulations governing 'children at nurse' were probably the only specific legislative responsibilities that were assigned to local authorities and their successors, the health boards. Typically, 'children at nurse' were those placed privately in pre-adoptive foster homes by adoption societies, and the visitation by State officials was an important safeguard for them.

Certain provisions within the Act had become largely defunct, such as exposure to burning, cleansing of verminous children, or acceptance of posessions for pawning from persons under the age of fourteen. Yet I managed to fall foul of the section disallowing children to be present in brothels. While on holiday in Canada, my wife entrusted me with the sole responsibility for our children for one night while she fulfilled a social engagement elsewhere. For dinner I brought them to the Hot and Spicy Emporium, mistaking a strip club for a Chinese restaurant.

To enforce child protection, we used the sections of the Act to do with assault, ill treatment and neglect. Using this Edwardian yardstick, we shoehorned the legislation to fit the circumstances of the case when we had taken a decision that parents were not fit to care for their children. These cases were heard in the Children's Court, and if the judge agreed with our assessment, we were awarded a fit persons order. The health boards where we social workers worked were the designated fit persons, so this gave us the authority to place the child in a residential or foster care setting. These orders usually lasted until the child reached the age of majority.

There was another, more innocuous section, referring to improper guardianship. We used this when we didn't have sufficient evidence of one big incident that would clearly demonstrate ill treatment or assault. It applied particularly to cases of neglect, which is more insidious and pernicious. Neglect has to be viewed as a process rather than an event because its harmful effects only manifest themselves over time, like a progressive disease. When presenting these cases to the court, we knitted together a compilation of venial sins which, when aggregated, amounted to one big mortal sin.

*

Eileen was an improper guardian. She had two children – a girl aged eight and a boy aged six. A highly strung alcoholic, Eileen had been recently widowed when I first met her. Her partner had been shot dead just before I took over the case.

He answered his hall door to a masked man who calmly shot him in front of Eileen and the children. Witnesses described the gunman walking away with the gun barrel resting on his shoulder, like a weary labourer after a hard day's work.

The family lived in an enclosed block of flats off Sheriff Street. Walking in, I could feel all the eyes as I deciphered the numbers and letters on the doors. An old woman sitting on a chair outside her door shouted over to me, 'Who are you looking for son?' She directed me to the Eileen's flat, laying back in contentment now that she had gotten the low-down.

There were no lifts so I walked up two external flights of stairs which led on each level to balconies fronting rows of hall doors. On the turn of the first flight, I gagged at the caustic stink of stale urine. On the next level a group of little kids in underpants were squirting each other with water from old washing-up liquid bottles. 'Who are you looking for mister?'

'You're alright,' I said as I looked for the door number.

'Well fuck off yourself', one of them shrugged, with a water squirt in my direction.

I knocked on the door, which was wide open. 'What?' came from deep within. So much angst crammed into the one little word. I introduced myself. There was no response, so I stepped into the hallway. From there I could see straight down into the kitchen. Eileen was at the big kitchen sink with her back to me. There was something in it, which I couldn't make out at first. As I came to the kitchen door I could see a little boy sitting in the sink. He peeped out from behind his mother, his thick black hair plastered to his white face. He purposefully excavated his nose with his forefinger as his mother scoured his back with a course cloth. His ribs stuck out under the taut, pale skin like a chicken carcass. These flats were built in the mid-1940s with toilets but without bathrooms, the theory being that tenants would avail of the local public baths for a weekly wash. They were actually a good example of twentieth-century public housing, and were certainly a huge step-up from the tenements which they replaced.

Eileen had thin brown hair, cut short like a boy. She wore a light summer dress with a loud pattern that might have worked better as a curtain. I knew from the file that she was twenty-five, but she looked old. I wondered what convergence of fate had brought us together and why was I visiting her and not she visiting me? On the face of it we had a lot in common. We were the same age, Dubliners and northsiders. Yet even though we grew up only a few parishes apart, they might have been planets such was the actual difference between us. I was still in school, a tittering teenager in a blazer blagging about sexual ambitions, when she was having her first child. Now she was a mother of two and already a widow. Officially she was a single mother – an *innupta* as the public health nurses used to call them, from the Latin referring to the absence of nuptials.

Following the birth of her second child, Eileen was allocated the Corporation flat where she now lived. Prior to his death, the children's father came and went. As a colleague used to say, when the going gets tough the men get going. In any event, he had to lay low from officialdom or she would never be prioritised for housing as an unmarried mother.

'Well, get to it', Eileen growled, barely looking up from scrubbing the child. She had had the Welfare on her case before. I nodded towards the boy. She towelled him down quickly, dressed him, and told him to go out and play.

I beat about the bush. Fresh out of college and childless, it wasn't easy to confront a parent with a criticism of their child-rearing ability without sounding like an imposter. In my last year at college in Jordanstown, we used to do mock interviews on Friday afternoons. These were videoed and the whole class would then provide feedback on your interviewing skills. More often than not, I dodged it and got the early train back to Dublin. But the train wasn't the main attraction, it was the avoidance of the stage fright I suffered every time I put myself through the role plays.

So now I was in Eileen's kitchen, without the benefit of all those dress rehearsals. An agent of the State with a message to deliver on its behalf. Eileen had to pull her socks up or else. I managed to politely suggest we had received reports from the school. 'What sort of reports?' she snapped. 'Unfavourable ones', I gulped. I fumbled through the list I had practiced back at the office. The children were constantly late for school, usually hungry and dirty, and often dozed off in class. I had seen them myself on a visit to the school to observe them. Neighbours had also told the public health nurse that she was going out drinking in the evenings, leaving the kids alone. That got to her. Those sneaky fucking neighbours gawking from behind their curtains but never saying a word to her face. At least it directed her anger away from me.

In the months that followed I developed a reasonably good working relationship with Eileen. She admitted to being stressed out, that the kids were getting to her and that she was drinking every day to calm herself down. She couldn't afford it anyway so she had to go shoplifting to supplement her Unmarried Mother's Allowance. What would happen the kids if she got caught? She confided one day, 'I wish I could, like, take all the thoughts out of my head and spread them out on the table like a jigsaw.' Taking her cue, I offered to make an appointment for her to have an assessment at the local psychiatric outpatients clinic. She was insulted, castigating me and the Welfare and those bastard neighbours and the sneaky teachers. I retreated to the office.

But I was back about four weeks later with more complaints from the neighbours about her drunkenness and leaving the children on their own. The school also confirmed that they were as hard up as ever. We organised a case conference to bring all the key players together to pool information and come up with an agreed plan for the case.

On the day of the case conference, the GP was invited but didn't come. Nothing new there – it was impossible to get a general practitioner to attend a meeting. The children's teachers and their principal came. So too did the community welfare officer, who dispensed supplementary welfare payments to hardship cases, and in that capacity he knew Eileen well. A local community youth worker also came. He had good local knowledge and was tuned in to what the neighbours were saying among themselves. Lastly there was the area medical officer (the doctor in the health centre who does developmental checks and immunisations), who had seen the children recently.

The teachers were of the opinion that the children were suffering and should have been taken into care long ago. It is a virtual law in child protection – a case that will keep a teacher awake all night will be taken with a pinch of salt by a social worker the following morning. The teachers' view had to be backed up with proper evidence of neglect and not just a generalised concern. They were able to give concrete examples of the children being constantly late, dirty and nodding off in class, and regularly having little or no lunch. The community welfare officer had recently smelled drink on Eileen when she approached him for some cash to put towards the electricity arrears. The community worker said neighbours were concerned that Eileen was leaving the kids alone a lot at night. The area medical officer said the boy, the youngest child, was far behind on developmental milestones.

For my part, I knew that the children were going hungry. There was never much evidence of proper food in the flat. The previous Christmas I brought a ham to keep them going. After the holiday she said that she hadn't a pot big enough for the ham so she threw it down the rubbish shoot on the balcony. I also got skates for her to give to the kids. When I remarked that they were always in them she told me that was because they had no shoes.

Altogether there was probably enough evidence of ongoing neglect to go for a care order, but it was agreed to give Eileen one last chance. When I called around she wouldn't let me in so I had to deliver the ultimatum on my knees through her letter box. Either she agreed to go to the outpatients for an assessment or we were going to apply for a court order to have the children placed in care. There was no response. I went back to the office and started to prepare a report to be sent to the law agents. Next step would be an application to the Children's Court and a summons for Eileen to appear as the defendant.

But next morning Eileen called into the office and asked for me, hopping from one foot to the other like she needed the bathroom. Refusing to go into an office to talk, she just said, 'Alright, I'll do it', then turned and walked out. Taking the cue, I made an appointment in the clinic and dropped it through her letterbox. But that was the end of the spoon-feeding. She would now have to demonstrate some commitment by attending on the right day and at the right time.

And she did. Dissolving after the first five minutes with the psychiatrist, she spilled out all her troubles like a penitent to a priest. By the end of the session she had agreed go to St Dymphna's Alcoholic Treatment Unit on the North Circular Road. The programme typically involved detoxification, three weeks residential treatment in the form of individual and group therapy, then outpatient follow-up.

When the time came, her mother agreed to mind the children but not before making a big deal out of it. She wasn't well, but a couple of weeks wasn't going to kill her. On the day of her admission, I drove Eileen to St Dymphna's. She carried her things in a black refuse sack which she kept on her knees. I didn't go in with her – she needed to do that on her own. I told her I'd visit in a week or so when she'd settled but in the meantime I'd be on the phone to her therapist. 'I need a fucking drink', she whispered as she grabbed her things and made for the door.

When I visited her the following week, I was shown into a small waiting room with a battered mahogany table surrounded by an assortment of rickety chairs. On the wall a framed piece of embroidery pronounced that *Sobriety is a journey, not a destination.'* When Eileen was sent for and she burst in the door with, 'That fucking therapist is trying to get inside my head!' I said something like that was the general idea. She had obviously been waiting for me, angry and anxious, and I was going to get both barrels: 'Don't get smart with me – this isn't funny. You've no idea what I've been going through. That fucker said in front of everybody that I wasn't a good parent. And he said that you told him.'

I mumbled something about there being no corners in which to hide on the programme. But the door was always open and that she was there of her own free will.

'Free will my arse', Eileen cried. She had been put into a corner. Threatened. Either she finish the programme or her kids would be taken off her. What sort of free will was that? And that was it – she walked out.

Cursing my ham-fisted inexperience, I dropped into the therapist and told him how things had bombed. 'Listen', he said, 'if Eileen is going to make it in here she's going to have to face reality. It suits her down to the ground to use you as a scapegoat. As long as she's blaming you, she doesn't have to blame herself for anything.'

It made me feel better, but that night Eileen packed her things and used that open door.

When I started to write a social report for court I realised that I didn't actually know the children – not really. Nowadays children are consulted and their views are taken into account. They are asked what they want, even though it may not be what they need. The judge might even have a quiet word with them in chambers. But back in the late 1970s, the children were inanimate objects in this discourse and all contact was with the mother. She either stopped drinking or the children would be taken into care.

Had they been asked, they might have described getting themselves out to school in the morning while their mother slept the drink off. Coming home to those men drinking beer and watching telly and looking at them funny. The empty fridge and the cornflake dinners. Neighbours giving them scraps, like the seagulls out in the yard below the flat. Putting themselves to bed and those noises out on the balcony like robbers trying the door. And not building up your hopes when mammy said she'd do something, because she forgets things a lot. For all that, they would have said that they were mad about her and their granny, and school and their friends and the playground. And they could not have even imagined having all that taken away from them in one cataclysmic moment.

We got the fit persons order. There was enough evidence based on the combined testimony of the teacher, who refused to be a witness until she was summoned, the area medical officer and myself. The order would last for ten and thirteen years respectively. Eileen took the stand and didn't do herself any favours by ranting about the lack of support from health, social and educational services. But when she agreed with the solicitor for the health board that she had left rehab early, I could see the judge signing the order even before she left the stand.

Eileen disappeared after the hearing and we had to go around to the flats on our own to round up the children. A short-term foster home was already arranged for them. The children were walking in the gates of the flats after school when we arrived. The eldest saw me and knew. She hesitated, seemed to think about running, but then stopped with her chin on her chest. By the time I reached her she was sobbing. There was no possibility of consoling her, so we just put the two of them in the back of the car and drove them away.

8

'Jump...'

'Jump, you bastard', is what the man shouted up at Tony as he sat on the balcony six floors up, legs dangling over the side. Afterwards, he swore he was only having a laugh – he never thought he'd actually do it. He said he had seen Tony perched like that before. It annoyed him a bit because he thought he was just messing. Now he couldn't get the image of the fall and the impact and the carnage out of his mind. Guilt and horror would not be purged as he tried to rationalise the incident.

'Maybe he just fell', he reasoned, 'You can never be sure'. I didn't say anything but I knew – Tony's girlfriend told me he had talked of jumping before. He would brood for hours on the balcony looking down, not talking, leaning over, his white knuckles glued to the railing. Then, it seemed, the man's taunting became the tipping point.

Tony was eighteen, which meant I had known him for ten years. I hadn't seen him since he left care and went off the radar for a while. I'd heard he was back in the old neighbour-hood but I hadn't come across him. Still, I remembered his first admission to care very well. His father, a complete stranger, marched into the office and said he wanted to admit him. 'None of those court orders,' he said, 'Just voluntary care for a bit until I get things sorted out.' The family had recently come from the UK. I went through the usual rigmarole about alternatives to care such as family support, advice, help with the rent, to keep the family together. But this guy knew his way around the system: 'Just give him to the nuns for a few months. He'll be fine', he said. When I continued to resist, he got up and left abruptly with the child. I thought that was that – I didn't even know where they were staying. But the next day one of the social workers was coming back to the office from lunch when he found Tony on the doorstep, his schoolbag crammed with stuff. The father had just left him there, like a refugee.

We placed Tony in a children's home within a convent on the outskirts of town. We gave him to the nuns as the father had wanted, and, as far as we could tell, he was indeed fine as he had also predicted. At the age of eight Tony was already a care system veteran. There was no outward sign of panic or upset that we would expect to see in a child his age. The following day, after he had settled in, I visited Tony and took some history. He was one of three children. His older sisters had come back from the UK as well but they were setting up home on their own. The eldest was nineteen and she had had enough of her father – the drinking, the squabbling, the moving all the time. She brought the youngest girl with her, but there was no place for Tony.

His mother was dead – he wasn't sure how long. She was sick, in bed a lot and then she died. Among his few possessions was a crumpled picture of the Sacred Heart, which he took out and showed me. 'She gave that to me', he said and then put it back in the bottom of his bag. Before she died, they lived in a flat somewhere in Dublin, which he couldn't name or describe. It was only after she died that they started moving about a lot. He didn't seem to understand the concept of extended family because he couldn't identify any grandparents, uncles, aunts or cousins. He could only name his dad and two sisters. He was a bright child who had obviously had consistent schooling. He was clean and tidy and used to washing and dressing himself – hallmarks of an institutional upbringing.

From the description Tony gave us we learned that they had all been squeezed into a caravan on one of the canals.

They weren't Travellers – the caravan was just a temporary and pragmatic accommodation solution. Although it turned out the father fancied himself as a bit of a gypsy king – a wandering rover traveling wherever fancy took him. I eventually tracked him down to a site on the Royal Canal near Cabra. As I approached, his exact location was hard to miss because the caravan was on fire. Flames and toxic smoke funnelled high into the evening sky. I was shocked – first by the sight in front me and then by his reaction. He was frolicking about with a flagon in his hand, like he was at a beach party. Laughing like a loon, in between swigs he told me that he deliberately set the caravan on fire. He said he was on his own now and he didn't need any address, not even a trailer. He literally made a bonfire of his troubles and watched them blaze away.

Safe to say, this man was not impressing me as an ideal parent. We would normally look for alternative carers within the extended family if it looked like a child could not return home, so I went looking for the older sister, Helen. I traced her to a private flat in town. She didn't bat an eyelid at her father's antics, saying that he does a lot of crazy things when he has enough drink in him. Helen was economical with information but did tell me about her mother's death and how the father uprooted them immediately after. They were living in Dolphin's Barn, having a fairly normal life until her mother's illness. She was the main carer – the father came and went, getting himself in trouble occasionally for drunk and disorderly and other misdemeanours. The mother was diagnosed with cancer and died rather quickly before they had even adjusted to the fact that she was ill. Soon after her death, the father packed up and moved them all to England without any obvious plan.

The three children soon found themselves in care for the first time, placed together in a children's home. After a couple of months the father came for them – not through the front door but around the back during the night. Various other care placements ended the same way, or by the children absconding to meet the father by arrangement. They were on the run from social services, which is why they ended up back in Ireland.

Helen refused to consider taking Tony, saying she had more than enough on her plate with the sister. She was supportive of her father's plan to leave Tony in residential care for a few months. A few nights later, I was drinking with a friend in a pub in town when in walked Helen with a collection box. She was collecting for homeless girls (presumably herself and the sister), and when she saw me across the bar she turned and exited abruptly.

Months went by and Tony was still in residential care. Normally we would be considering foster care if the placement looked like it was going to be long-term. But Tony was different. He was quite settled in his residential placement and doing well in school. Far from being cowed by the staff he had a rather regal attitude, treating them like the help. 'It's your job to look after me,' he would say if he was ever challenged about doing chores about the house.

I did some life story work with him. This entailed preparing an album with photos and drawings associated with his life to date, in order to make sense of it and to preserve some of the memories. He had no family photos. We visited the house in Dolphin's Barn where he had lived and his old school, taking photos for the life story book. I made contact with social services in England and they sent over some school reports and pictures. He opened up a little about his mother. Although he didn't express it, her absence was a gaping wound. The loss, combined with his father's unreliability, left a stone in his heart. His true feelings were impermeable behind the tough exterior which he presented to the world.

I found out where his mother was buried and I brought him to visit her. He had never been back since the day she was buried. As part of the preparation, I had done an earlier visit, so that I could lead him straight to her. There was no headstone so I was relying on a graveyard plan provided by the undertakers. The plot was overgrown and unkempt so I tidied it up a bit for him. On the day, he made a card to place on her grave. It was a woman with a smiling face under a golden sun. He showed no outward sign of emotion but chatted, and even laughed a little, about everyday family things before everything started

Hanged If You Do...

to unravel. But when it was time to go he lingered, his face like a dam holding back a flood. 'What is it?' I asked. 'I can't remember her face,' he said.

His father had been living in hostels since the caravan fire, but he was getting sick of it. He looked for my help to get him onto the council housing list. He said if he got a place he would take the two youngest children back. I wasn't at all sure about that as a viable plan, but I agreed to help him. I soon discovered that he owed sizeable rent arrears on the previous family home which, I learned, he just abandoned by posting the key in through his own letterbox. It was a tall order to get him back on the list. I started by tapping various charitable trusts for help with the arrears. Then I wrote to the council saying we were anxious to reunite the family. After a long time he got a two-bedroom flat back in Dolphin's Barn. It was at a time when there were a lot of drugs in the area and local vigilantes were keeping an eye on things. They paid him a visit, welcomed him to the area, set out the community ground rule of no drugs, saying they would be back if they had any cause for concern. But his drug of choice came in a bottle, which was perfectly socially acceptable.

I paid him a visit after he was a few weeks in the flat. He had put it together well with odds and ends from charities and second-hand shops. When I asked him if he was drinking much, he replied, 'Well, if you'd put a barrel of Guinness in front of me there, I'd drink it.' A few nights later he was sitting by the fire, drinking by himself in the flat. He put the poker into the coals and, when it was red hot, he took it out and branded his cheek with it.

The family was very disjointed, each of the four of them living lives parallel to each other. None of them were good at visiting Tony – a month or more could go by before any one of them would call in to see him. The prospect of him going back to the father was remote – neither was he pushing for it. We were happy enough to let the voluntary care arrangement continue on that basis. Rather than cause unnecessary upset by going to court for a care order, the placement went on like that for a few years.

One day, out of the blue, the father dropped in to tell me Helen had died. I couldn't process the news, thinking it must be some sort of twisted plot. But it was true. The circumstances were vague – she died in her sleep, apparently from asphyxia. She had asthma and I knew she took a lot of pills unrelated to her condition. She had been going the rounds among GPs and pharmacies in order to maximise her prescriptions. But this was a complete blindside.

Then came the next shock – she was already buried. He said he didn't want Tony to know yet – his other daughter had moved in with him and he wanted that to settle down before he told him. He said Tony might feel left out. I remember how my voice quivered as I struggled to present a veneer of professionalism, when all I wanted to do was smack him. In the end I gave him twenty-four hours to tell Tony or I would.

We rehearsed how he would break the news, a teaspoon at a time – there was bad news, something had happened to Helen, she had gone to bed and so on. I went with him and the other sister to the children's home unannounced, so Tony knew something was up. As soon as he walked into the visitors' room the father, despite my coaching and his promises, blurted out, 'Helen is dead.' It took a moment for the brick to hit Tony, but then he just ran out of the room without another word being spoken by anyone. I could see him grab a bike from the shed and he just cycled off. He was gone for hours.

My tolerance of the father expired that day. We prepared a case to bring to the Children's Court and care orders were granted in respect of both children. The sister was placed with Tony and they remained together in that children's home until they were discharged when they both reached eighteen. The father went back to England and, after a couple of years, was never heard of again. I tried to trace him via the Salvation Army, who helped with missing persons, but no luck. Then I moved jobs and, as often happens, the relationship with the children was severed and they had to start all over with a new social worker.

Years later, I heard Tony had left care and I was glad to think he was getting by in the real world. I had vague plans

Hanged If You Do...

to go and see him but news of his death arrived before I did anything about it. I felt guilty – not that I hadn't visited but because all those years in the care system had not equipped him, socially or personally, for life as an independent adult. The State removed him from his father but, in the end, had it done any better than he would have?

Tony was staying with his girlfriend at the time his death. By all accounts it was a superficial enough relationship, but she was still very upset by what had happened in her flat. I introduced myself to her at the funeral and called to see her a few days after. She had all Tony's stuff, which didn't amount to much. I was reminded of the time he was left at the office door with nothing but his schoolbag and the clothes he stood up in. She showed me the life storybook which we had done and he had kept for all those years. There was a photo of my old car that we took the day we visited his mother's grave – the one he now shares with her. In between the pages was the crumpled picture of the Sacred Heart, causing the girlfriend to raise a curious eyebrow. 'His mother gave it to him,' I explained.

9

'A Bit of Incest...'

*I*n 1981, I was preparing two sisters for their return home from care. They were fifteen and sixteen and had spent the past four years in a residential unit. It was a purpose-built home on the grounds of a convent. As the orphanages were decanted, many were replaced on the same site by smaller 'family style' homes. There were six or seven children in residence, with as many staff and another unit right next door. This was in a salubrious part of town and the girls, who were from the inner city, had acquired some of the attributes of their current environment, including the accent. They fitted in well in the local convent school, sang in the choir and attended ballet. They were in no rush to move back home. In fact, they were reluctant. It was their father who was pushing. Their mother had died a few years previously and the father lived alone in the flat. He had a full-time job and was well able to support them. There were older siblings – two sisters with children of their own and a brother whom I had never met.

I wasn't long involved in the case and the decision for the girls to go home had already been taken. It fell to me to follow through with the plan. I spoke with them a lot about the move. It seemed to me that they had become a bit snobby and didn't want to let go of the niceties of their middle-class lifestyle. I arranged for them to continue all the extracurricular activities they had enjoyed in the children's home. It was agreed that they would move home during the summer holidays. As part of the preparation, they spent several Saturdays and the occasional overnight in the flat. They loved their little nephews and nieces and ultimately that was a draw for them in going along with the plan.

Days before the move, I was in the Social Work Department writing up the file when a more experienced colleague leaned over to me. 'Just so you know', he said, 'there was a bit of incest in that family at one stage.' As a citizen I knew what incest was, but throughout my social work training and until then in practice it had never even been whispered. I went back over the file. The reason for admission to care was put down to a fraught marital relationship together with excessive drinking on the father's part, both of which were taking their toll on the girls. I approached the older sisters and asked if there was any reason I should be concerned about the girls going home. 'Absolutely not,' they said and were concerned about any last-minute backtracking. So the girls moved home in the summer as planned. They became very involved with their sisters and their little children, spending a good bit of time there. Their introduction into the local secondary school went well and they made new friends easily. I was relieved about that.

Then around the end of October, I got a call from one of the older sisters who wanted to see me straight away. The girls told her that their father was interfering with them. She said the same had happened to her at their age. I was flabbergasted that she was only telling me now. She said she thought that was all in the past. I met with the girls. They said that at night their father was starting to hover around their bedroom door. Sometimes he would come into the room and start to grope them as they pretended to sleep. They began to lock the bedroom door when they went to bed at night. The previous evening, the father had come home drunk. When he tried the door and found it locked he went crazy. He jemmied the door to access the girls.

We arranged for them to stay with their sister that night and I went around to the father. The debris from the broken doorway was still on the floor. He readily admitted what he had done but explained that he only got the urge when he had been drinking. His description was of a man possessed, who had no control over his emotions or his actions. In the end, the girls went to live between their sisters while the father stayed on his own in the flat. The criminal aspect of what he had done never even crossed my mind.

*

At a time when child protection services were entirely preoccupied with physical abuse, or non-accidental injury as we then called it, the concept of sexual abuse was literally unheard of. The first inkling of a professional response came in 1982, when Christine Hennessy, a colleague from the Social Work Department in Killarney Street, went to the Sacramento Child Abuse Project. She was followed the next year by Kieran McGrath, who went on to specialise in services for child victims of sexual abuse. In 1983, the Irish Association of Social Workers (IASW) organised a seminar on incest. This was the first opportunity for a broad audience of social workers, and other professionals, to educate themselves on the subject.

Following the IASW seminar the Department of Health asked Irish Council for Civil Liberties (ICCL) to set up a working party on child sexual abuse. It was 1988 before the ICCL report was published but, through its efforts, the working party raised professional awareness of the prevalence of sexual abuse. In 1983, the Department of Health issued revised guidelines on the management of non-accidental injury. Passing reference was made to sexual abuse, where it was described as a possible cause of physical injury. While the reference was slight, it was nevertheless the first official acknowledgement of sexual abuse as an abuse category. The following year, 1984, the department included sexual abuse in its data collection and statistics.

Pennies started to drop for me in relation to past cases where I wasn't quite sure what was going on. While still in the psychiatric services, I had come across a teenager who was a selective mute. This was a recognised anxiety disorder where someone is known to have the capacity to talk but will not in certain situations. The girl I was dealing with would not talk at all. I met her and her parents in their home. The father was domineering, controlling and possessive. The mother was passive and docile. With the wisdom of hindsight, it seemed so obvious to me that what the girl wasn't saying was that she was being sexually abused by her father.

In 1985, the Sexual Assault and Treatment Unit (SATU) was established in the Rotunda Maternity Hospital. Although established in response to the needs of adults, it soon began to accept referrals regarding children. It was headed up by Dr Moira Woods, whose qualifications were in general practice. She was pretty much a one-person band. She developed assessment techniques using anatomically correct dolls and age-appropriate drawing materials, and was skilled at communicating with children. Following the development of social work connections with Sacramento, we social workers also used these materials, but the SATU role expanded and in the end we just referred children there rather than conduct assessments ourselves.

*

An early referral I made to the SATU was of two sisters, aged around eight and nine years. Both their parents had a mental disability. In addition, he drank and she had a psychotic illness. There were a lot of unsavoury visitors to the flat at all hours of the day and night. The eldest girl started to manifest some sexualised behaviour that concerned me, so I referred them both to the SATU. First I had to get their parents' agreement. Getting them to say yes was easy – but getting them to understand, thereby giving informed consent, was another matter.

I brought the children to see Dr Woods in the Rotunda and waited outside while she did her assessment. After a while she called me into the room. She invited the children to show me what they had told her. Using printouts of child-friendly human shapes they indicated, one after the other in self-conscious achievement, where their daddy had touched them. It was not what I was expecting, but there it was. They were clearly demonstrating sexual abuse by their father.

Dr Woods said they couldn't be left in that environment and should be taken into care immediately. That was my call, but I was influenced by her level of concern. I brought the children home, but went immediately to confer with the senior social worker. I then got on to the solicitors for the health board. It was concluded that there were grounds for a place of safety order, an emergency provision to remove the children on summary evidence before the District Court. A full hearing would then follow.

I got the order and arrived back at the flat late that after-noon with a carload of gardaí. I knocked on the door and the gardaí presented the order to the parents. As the import of what I was saying began to dawn on them, they naturally became agitated and upset. The father lunged at me as the gardaí stood between us. The mother just whimpered silently. I went looking for the children. I found them in a wardrobe in their parents' bedroom, where they had gone to hide when the shouting started. I led them out by the hand. They walked compliantly with me past their parents, as the gardaí held their father back.

We went out and down the three fights of steps to the close below. A garda leaned on the bonnet of the squad car, admiring his fingernails. My car was parked behind. A small group of neighbours looked on as I put the children in the back seat. They were aghast, as if I had brought the children out in body bags. Then their father appeared, breaking free from the gardaí, and running towards the car. Two gardaí wrestled him to the ground and held him there. 'Harrison, you bastard', I heard him scream as I drove his children away. Neither the parents nor the children had any idea of where I was bringing them.

I brought them to Madonna House, a large children's home in Blackrock run by the Sisters of Charity. It was set out in campus style with individual units clustered around the grounds. Staff liked a brisk handover of the children, rather than a lingering and tearful farewell. They would then be bathed and freshly clothed. So I left abruptly, promising the children that I would be back in the morning. When I returned the next day, the eldest girl was hiding behind the door from this omnipotent social worker who had plucked her out of her world without warning.

*

Years later I saw in the media that Dr Woods was found guilty by the Medical Council of professional misconduct arising from allegations made by some families regarding their treatment by her in the 1980s. A finding was made that she was effectively in sole charge of the unit without adequate medical supervision and that she had no formal training in the management of paediatric victims of sexual assault. The Medical Council was critical of the Rotunda and pointed out the broader responsibilities of hospital authorities to oversee doctors in their employment. In response, Dr Woods said that she did not agree with the findings and that she was only ever motivated by the best interest of the children. There can be little dispute about that. She was a pioneer in an entirely new area of practice which sought to better understand child sexual abuse. A hazard for any pioneer is the risk of losing direction, but invariably they make it much easier for others to follow after them.

In 1987, the Department of Health took a decision to establish child sexual abuse assessment units in the Children's Hospital, Temple Street and Our Lady's Hospital in Crumlin. These were headed up by consultant child psychiatrists, the first being Dr Carol Fitzpatrick in Temple Street and Dr Imelda Ryan in Crumlin. In addition to the psychiatrists, the teams comprised two social workers and two psychologists. The remit of the units was to provide a broad-based assessment which considered the sexual abuse in the context of the overall psycho-social needs of the family. With these units in place the SATU was able to revert to its original intention of treating adults.

The approach taken by the new assessment units in the children's hospitals made for calmer decision-making regarding child protection. I cannot recall any emergency admission to care arising from an assessment in either unit. When cases did go to court, judges valued the expert opinion of staff in the assessment units. In predictable hierarchical fashion, the psychiatrist was preferred, followed in turn by the psychologists, then the hospital social workers. On the bottom of the heap were the child protection workers in the community, even though they were the key workers in every case. This eventually had the effect of deskilling child protection social workers. While we originally did this work in the social work departments, it became a specialism, resulting in all sexual abuse assessments being referred to the units.

It was a good move to place the assessment units in children's hospitals, but arguably there would have been further advantages in placing them in community-based health and social service settings. After all, the children did not require hospitalisation. No such pedestal was created for physical abuse, emotional abuse or neglect. Here, social workers continued to have autonomy and their evidence continued to be sought by the courts. Where medical evidence was required, particularly in cases of non-accidental injury, it was usually social workers who did the running in terms of acquiring specialist medical opinion.

The Department of Health issued new child abuse guidelines in 1987. This time they were sufficiently cognisant of sexual abuse, both in terms of its recognition and the multidisciplinary nature of the work. The department's own statistics had shown that over the period 1984–1987, child sexual abuse referrals had increased by almost 1,000 per cent. Then the notion that sexual abuse was committed by strangers was blown out of the water when Robbie Gilligan and Dr Kieran McKeown published findings on the prevalence of child sexual abuse in the Eastern Health Board region in 1988. It found that 60 per cent of abusers were related to the child victim. They also highlighted that a large proportion of sexual abusers were adolescents.

It is still the case today that one-third of all sexual abuse is perpetrated by young people under eighteen years. Most of the abuse is within the perpetrator's own family. Kieran McGrath, who originally went to Sacramento in the early 1980s, returned in 1990. By this time, he was working in the assessment unit in Temple Street and recognised that young people required interventions tailored to suit their age group. He brought back and, in association with colleagues, amended the Sacramento model to suit Irish conditions. The Northside Inter-Agency Project (NIAP) was established to provide an inter-agency and multi-disciplinary programme, providing a community-based treatment programme to young people between the ages of thirteen and eighteen years. It was originally established on a grant of £50 each from the Eastern Health Board, the Mater Hospital and Temple Street. It relied, and continues to rely, on colleagues from different agencies coming together in the evening to give their time and expertise to the project. In time, the Southside Inter-Agency Project (SIAT) was established to cater for that part of Dublin.

Social workers can take considerable credit for raising awareness of child sexual abuse in the first instance. Then they did something about it, such as the educational inputs from Sacramento, the first seminar on incest, participation in assessment services and the establishment of treatment services. In the early 1980s, child sexual abuse was an unspoken, virtually unknown phenomenon. But by 1988 it had become, and remains, a primary focus of child protection social work. Within one decade, we had moved from a 'bit of incest' to an avalanche of child sexual abuse which still has child protection social work snowed in.

10

Drugs and Deals

*I*n February 1982, Tony Gregory, north-inner-city activist and city councillor, was elected to Dáil Éireann on his second time out. It was a hell of an achievement considering his political opponents in that constituency of Dublin North Central. There was Bertie Ahern, future Taoiseach; George Colley, former Tánaiste; Michael Keating, a popular Fine Gael TD; and Michael O'Leary, leader of the Labour Party, who came in behind Tony.

Gregory's election was at the expense of Alice Glenn, a conservative member of Fine Gael. The first woman to chair the Eastern Health Board where I worked, Glenn was pro-life, anti-communist, anti-divorce and anti-contraception. She eventually left Fine Gael because it wasn't conservative enough for her at a time when its leader, Garret FitzGerald, was peddling a liberal agenda. She is reported to have asked, 'what man would have anything to do with a woman who has been used and abused by a man who comes along with a condom?' But Gregory's election was where the rubber hit the road because, when the votes were counted, he held the balance of power.

What happened next has entered the annals of political folklore. The three main political leaders came courting for his vote. But it was Charles J. Haughey, leader of Fianna Fáil and would-be Taoiseach, who really committed to the process. To negotiate the deal, Haughey invited Gregory to his estate in Kinsealy, but Gregory insisted that all the meetings take place in his offices in Summerhill Parade. Tony Gregory was accompanied primarily by his brother Noel, Mick Rafferty, local community activist, and our own Fergus McCabe from the Eastern Health Board, albeit fully embedded as a community activist himself. It was a source of great glee for us to see Fergus in his famous duffle coat in the newspapers and on television, holding his own with the political elite.

For the final session Haughey arrived alone, leaving Bertie Ahern outside in the car. He opened with the now legendary remark, 'Well lads, you know what I want. The question is, what do you want?' Gregory had a paper ready, albeit a necessarily rushed job without any great detail or costings. The demands were very broad-ranging but focused in on housing, employment and education. There was a lesser section on children and families. Picking up from the *Report of the Task Force on Child Care*, published in 1980, there were demands for a National Council for Children, the establishment of regional child care authorities, and an Oireachtas Committee on Child and Family Welfare. There were also demands for legislative change, including a new Children's Bill, reformation on adoption and the abolition of illegitimacy.

There was only a passing reference to tackling drug abuse and the provision of treatment services. The wildfire of the heroin epidemic was just a glowing ember in early 1982– but it was a raging inferno by the end of that year. The issues of drug addiction, and their by-products of organised and petty crime, would preoccupy Tony Gregory's priorities for the remainder of his political career.

Altogether the initiatives amounted to a massive cash investment of about £80 million in full year costs into the north inner city. On 8 April 1982, the day before the vote for Taoiseach, Tony Gregory and Charles J. Haughty signed the 'Gregory Deal' in Summerhill Parade. Or, as we liked to refer to it thereafter,

'Summerhill Boulevard'. The following day Gregory voted for Haughey, who was in turn voted in as Taoiseach.

*

Heroin addiction spread through the inner city like a plague. It was the drug of choice for young people because it was potent and relatively cheap. An opiate web was draped across entire communities where scores of teenagers were entrapped in a network of drug use and petty crime to feed their habit. Organised criminals soon muscled in on this lucrative new market. Families and neighbourhoods were exposed to the inevitable violence which followed as debts were extracted and turf was protected.

Mainstream health and social services were slow to recognise and react to the emerging epidemic. I was a member of the Voluntary and Statutory Group for the Seán McDermott Street area, which saw the writing on the wall early on. That was because it comprised of people working on the ground in a confined area where everyone knew what was going on at street-by-street level. The so-called V&S met regularly to bridge voluntary and statutory into a cohesive and coordinated force. We knew this new phenomenon required a different approach to the traditional doctor–patient relationship if it was to be relevant to young people. Very soon after his election Tony Gregory, accompanied by some locals, met the Minister for Health, Dr Michael Woods. They presented the bones of a proposal for a local walk-in service for young people where they could access professional treatment services in their own neighbourhood.

To my amazement, I was asked to head up the project. I was chuffed and didn't have to think twice. It would be called the Talbot Project, after the Venerable Matt Talbot, renowned for his temperance and mortification of the flesh, but also for being a man of the people.

There was a lot of political heat to get things moving and, as I encountered many times since, corners were cut in the interest of expediency. The brass in the Eastern Health Board had given little thought to what the project would look like. The immediate objective was to be able to report to the Department of Health that a project had been set up, as requested by Tony Gregory of the fragile Government.

More experienced colleagues suggested to me that I look for a significant pay increase, given the additional responsibilities and the fact that the health board was on the back foot. I had to go and see Áine Flannagan, a senior administrator in headquarters with responsibility for addiction services. The former head of personnel, she was a formidable character who did not wear her seniority lightly. She told me I came highly recommended and that she was delighted that I had accepted the challenge. Buoyed by a newfound self-confidence I made my pitch for the pay claim. She looked me up and down in astonishment, like a goddess whose garment had been touched by a mortal. Then she said, 'This isn't Smurfits, you know.' My confidence deflated with my hopes. She said I would be entitled to an acting-up allowance which would come into effect straight away. It never did, straight away or otherwise.

We talked in broad terms about the objects of the project. It was very apparent that the powers that be had little time for all this community activism and participation. The established preference was for the old school where people who knew better did things to passive recipients of services. The Eastern Health Board headquarters was situated in Emmet House, Thomas Street in the south inner city. Heroin was becoming a big problem in the Liberties too. You could look out the windows of Emmet House into some of the flat complexes where heroin flourished. But geographic proximity was the only thing Emmet House had in common with its neighbours. There was no strategy, because there was still no full appreciation of the detrimental effect of this new public health phenomenon.

Back on the social work team there were rumblings that my post had not been opened up to competition, as would normally be the case with a new job or promotional opportunity, and talk about jobs for the boys. That hurt because I wasn't in cahoots with anyone. The union was called in. My case was not helped by the fact that the union had a point

– there should have been a competition. As it transpired, the union went easy on me and, after throwing a few shapes, let the issue fade away.

But that was only the beginning. I was on the phone to Tony Gregory about something or other. He took the opportunity to express his surprise that someone like me was appointed as project leader. Maybe through personal insecurity I took this to mean someone who is a mainstream professional, non-community, non-local, middle-class do-gooder such as myself. The vote of no confidence from the man with his finger on the button was a right kick in the guts. The elation I had felt just a few weeks before had dwindled to a sickening anxiety. Before I even got the project up and running I was the meat in the sandwich between the health board and the community leadership.

I cut myself off from the social work team because the project had to be seen as independent and neighbour-hood-based. From the health board's perspective, I was behind enemy lines. From mine, I was adrift in the community with no base, no marching orders and no budget. Years later, I read in Shane Butler's book, *Alcohol, Drugs and Health Promotion in Modern Ireland*, that a fund of £25,000 was allocated to the project. That was complete news to me. I scrounged around for some sort of a premises to work from. The parish had nothing and neither were there any offers from the community sector. Eventually, the local health board administrator let me use an office upstairs in Summerhill Health Centre. It was a dump, and useless as a reception for local young people, but beggars can't be choosers. I moved in with my few bits and pieces.

On my very first day in Summerhill I was robbed. I had left my jacket on the back of a chair with my wallet in it. A visiting opportunist, who did a quick scan of the upstairs, found the wallet. He was seen coming down the stairs and someone tipped me off. It was a young guy in his twenties who was in to see the community welfare officer. When he came out from community welfare, I confronted him. He did the usual, 'Are you accusing me of stealing?' I assured him that I was. He pushed past me with a few expletives and was gone. I could hardly have searched him.

The following day, I got the thief's address from the community welfare officer. He was living in a squat in a nearby Georgian terrace. I paid him a visit – or rather I paid a visit to his place when he wasn't there. It was just one room in a semi-derelict building. The door was unlocked. Pushing it in I saw a mattress on the floorboards, dragged into the corner of the empty room. There were no chairs or table – just a pile of clothes. On the bare walls on one side of the mattress were pinups of nude women. On the wall over the head of the mattress he had sellotaped a picture of the Sacred Heart. On the ceiling, ornate Georgian coving looked down on the sparse room that had seen better days. I thought of Louis McNiece's poem, which I had learned in school, about the bare bones of a fanlight over a hungry door. I poked about but there was no sign of the wallet. I hadn't come in expectation of finding it. I came to extract proportionate revenge by taking something from him of equivalent value to its contents. But there was nothing worth taking. So, in an admittedly petty act of restorative justice, I pissed on his bedding before I left.

*

Dr Michael Woods, Minister for Health, in the face of local claims of an escalating drugs problem, but without any counterbalancing intelligence from the Eastern Health Board, decided to commission some research of his own. He appointed the Medico-Social Research Board to undertake a study of the extent of the problem. Dr Geoffrey Dean was the director. Dr John Bradshaw was the field researcher, assisted by Fr Paul Lavelle, a Jesuit who was working as a local priest in Lourdes parish. I brought the two doctors around to meet some people and to get a sense of the neighbourhood. In their suits and ties they looked out of place. Dr Bradshaw was very concerned that nearly every service provider he met was a smoker. As addictions go, he was only warming up.

Over the course of several months, which brought them into the spring of 1983, they undertook a carefully executed survey. They found a 10 per cent prevalence of heroin addiction in young people aged between fifteen and twenty-four years. Nearly all the participants were both unemployed and daily users of heroin; 11 per cent were illiterate and just 4 per cent had any kind of educational certification. Within the confines of well-defined communities in the north inner city, there was the proof of a direct link between socio-economic hardship and heroin addiction.

The findings reinforced the need for a local service accessible to young people. Still, the only place I could see the young people was in the office in Summerhill. Teenagers had to get past the porter first and that meant knowing their business before they got in. Then 'interviewing' young people at my desk wasn't the thing. Jervis Street Treatment Centre started to send me young people they had come across from the area. Most of them didn't show up. Those who did wondered why they were there, and, a lot of the time, so did I.

I got on better with the younger kids. They were more amenable to letting me visit their parents and other family members. This led me to see at close range the devastation the young person's addiction was having on the whole family. Besides the actual drug addiction, heroin had to be bought. This led to daily rounds of shoplifting, pilfering and mugging. Then there were debts to pay – in money or blood.

The number of teenagers coming to see me never exceeded a trickle. There was little engagement with the project from the community sector and none from the health board. Occasionally, I would be wheeled out to board meetings to do a spin on how well it was all going, even though I knew better. Back then I had not yet learned that there is no such thing as a public service fairy godmother. You have to make things happen yourself.

After five or six months in the doldrums it was obvious to me that the project was just tokenism. The public health and social services system was still not grasping the fact that an epidemic was eating the inner city alive, and I was just fiddling with the problem. So I threw in the towel. It was a massive relief to get back to the social work team in Killarney Street, despite an underlying sense of failure.

My departure forced a rethink in relation to the future of the project. In an uninspired and probably retrogressive step, a senior social worker from the Drug Treatment Centre in Jervis Street took over. As Jervis Street was the mainstream service provider, this meant that they had simply opened a branch office in the north inner city. It was a long way from the original concept in the V&S meetings where community participation in the running of the project was envisaged. Yet, despite everything, the Talbot Project celebrated its thirtieth birthday in 2013. Unlike so many of the young people who attended over the years, it survived.

11

'Our Leah Has AIDS'

You couldn't be mad at Leah – not for long. She had the impish qualities of a mischievous child. I don't know how many times I told her not to turn up stoned for her monthly access visit to the children, but she did anyway. A small mercy was that she would always be mobile and upright, even if lethargic. The two girls, aged two and three, were in foster care. Her introduction was always the same. She would say to each of them in turn, 'Hello Chicken,' tickling them under the chin with her index finger. Then she would do the same to me.

The visits took place in a little room off the entrance hall of the Carnegie Trust Child Welfare Centre in Lord Edward Street. I liked working there because of the continuity of care which the building had provided since 1927. Built with funding from the Carnegie Trust, it was a resource to generations of Dubliners in the south inner city, where they could access health and social services. There was a long tradition of such provision from the building, dating back to the work of Lady Aberdeen, wife of the Lord Lieutenant, in the first decades of the twentieth century. She founded the National Health Association, dedicated to the eradication of tuberculosis, which was rampant in the Dublin slums at that time. A benefactor of the poor, she also organised the supply of clean milk to needy children, the construction of playgrounds, and campaigned for better housing and against excessive alcohol consumption by women.

What would Lady Aberdeen have made of the heroin epidemic and the associated emergence of HIV and AIDS? No doubt she would have taken the same no-nonsense approach with which she tackled TB, the scourge of her day. This was 1986, when we could have done with another champion like her. I had recently moved from the social work team in Killarney Street on the northside to Lord Edward Street on the southside. A noticeable difference between the two areas was that on the northside teenagers were using heroin, but on the southside the users were a bit older – in their twenties. This opened up the new scenario of parental addiction and the consequences of this for their children.

Meanwhile Leah's children were swinging around the pillars, just outside in the front hallway, to make themselves dizzy. It was hard to prevent access being an artificial encounter. But we did what we could with a few toys and some ragged reading material. Generally, Leah's visits went well. Her good nature meant there was never any aggro, as there often was during access visits in other cases. The girls always came with at least one of their foster carers, so they were secure and didn't mind Leah, even when she just plonked in a chair and dozed for the hour.

Most of the referrals to the social work service were coming from medical social workers in the Coombe and the maternity unit in St James' Hospital. Because of the high level of drug addicts of child-bearing age there was a well-established communication chain between our service, the maternity hospitals and the Drug Advisory and Treatment Services in Jervis Street Hospital. In this way the majority of addicts who became pregnant were picked up at the antenatal stage.

Most children and families were referred to our social work service because of parental neglect, but this was closely followed by parental drug addiction. Of course, there was a co-relationship because it is almost impossible to maintain a heroin addiction and a stable home life simultaneously. In recognition of this, in 1987 the Eastern Health Board provided our team with a new social work post specifically to deal with opiate-addicted parents. This was an insightful and innovative development, the credit for which goes to John Doyle and Fred Donohue, who were senior managers in the health board's Community Care Programme. Mick Lacey, a former student of mine and no stranger to the area, got the job.

The only way a mother who was using could manage as a parent was with the help of a stable partner or the assistance of the older generation. 'Granny power' became a thing in the south inner city where grandmothers became the primary carer in situations where new mothers continued, or resumed, their heroin usage after their baby was born. Another less common source of support were the fathers of these children, but they were almost always addicts too, only contributing to the chaos. By and large the fathers drifted like spectres in the shadows of family life, interested in sex but none of its consequences. Neither were they held much to account by social services. Invariably it was the mothers we social workers chased, harried and supervised.

Leah's mother was very supportive, but she was already caring for Leah's sister's three children. This older sister was a drinker and Leah's mother was already overstretched with parenting responsibilities, which is why Leah's children had ended up in care. Leah's boyfriend came and went. And now, during this access visit Leah announced, or let slip, that she was pregnant.

In the mid-1980s there was a huge information gap on the whole subject of AIDS among the public at large and health and social service professionals in particular. Consequently, plague talk reached biblical proportions. The condition only started to be detected in the early 1980s. In 1983, it emerged that the female partners of men had become infected, indicating that the virus could be spread through heterosexual sex. Then it became known that the sharing of needles in intravenous drug users was another source of infection. The first accounts of AIDS in children did not entirely rule out casual contact as the cause. Later it emerged that children could become infected *in utero* or via breast milk. Hence, in a grotesque inversion of

Hanged If You Do...

natural order, the womb and the breast became unsafe places for those infants of HIV-infected mothers.

We arranged for Leah to attend St James' antenatal clinic. She tested positive for HIV – the first person I knew to do so. All of us involved in her care were shocked and very uncertain about what to do next. The obstetrician, the medical social worker and I searched around for information, which was not yet forthcoming from the Department of Health. The three of us went to a gay men's health organisation, which was ahead of the posse. They were very helpful and informative and gave us a load of information leaflets to take away with us. I left a stack of them at reception in Lord Edward Street. A few days later they were discovered by the area administrator and removed.

I called around to Leah's mother to leave in some forms to sign. She was great at getting Leah to do things. 'Did you hear, our Leah has AIDS?', she asked as she slumped to the kitchen table, sick with worry. 'She doesn't have AIDS Mrs Kelly, she has the virus', I placated. 'It's all the one,' she whispered. 'Leah is done for, and that's it.' By the mid-1980s one in three intravenous drug users were HIV positive and they soon started to die. Mick Lacey, who had undertaken the role of addiction social worker, soon became an undertaker in a literal sense as a succession of young people's funerals were organised and attended.

There was as yet no absolute certainty of all the transmission routes for the virus, so there was still extreme caution in relation to it. Once I made coffee for Leah in Lord Edward Street as we discussed her pregnancy. She was afraid of dying, afraid for her children's future, afraid that she would infect her new baby before it was even born, and guilty that she had brought all this on her mother. When we were finished she offered to wash her cup. I wouldn't hear of it. But when she was gone I washed the two cups, then put the kettle on and scalded hers with boiling water.

In 1986, I wrote an article for the *Irish Social Worker* pondering the implications of AIDS on the reception of children into care. It hadn't happened yet, but it was only a matter of time before a HIV positive child would need to be admitted to care. From what we knew in other countries, half of HIV-infected newborn infants developed AIDS within two years. Opinion was divided on the best form of care for a HIV positive child. Some felt foster care was out of the question because there was still considerable fear about transmission routes. Should foster carers wear protective gloves while changing nappies? What about the risk to other children? And would those who come into contact with HIV positive children have a right to know? Then there was the issue of life expectancy.

If residential care was considered a safer alternative should the parents of the other children be advised, and how would that go down? Should teachers be informed and, if so, who should they tell? I argued that haemophiliac children who contracted the virus were free to stay at home, go to school and engage in normal social activities – so why not a child in care? Nevertheless, there was great uncertainty and it was felt that it would take a super-human carer to take on a HIV positive child.

We weren't the only ones. I talked to a man who had just got out of prison, where he too tested positive for HIV. He described leper colony conditions in Mountjoy Prison. When testing was first introduced in the prison, anyone who tested positive was simply released. Then everybody wanted to be tested. So the prison set up an isolation unit with its own exercise yard and catering facilities. Prison officers were kitted with spacesuits and prisoners got disposable paper pillowcases and sheets. The dead were removed in body bags. According to this man, he first learned he was HIV positive when prison guards burst into his cell, cuffed him and took him to this segregated area.

Social stigma was a huge burden for the first carriers of the virus. There were even stories of families engaging in human segregation, such as the separation of cutlery, bedding and utensils. One girl I worked with took her own life. She had become very depressed and paranoid about who knew and what they were saying about her. Leaving her baby boy in the cot beside her, she left a note for her mother which ended, 'I'm dying anyway, but this way it's on my terms.'

Leah continued to use throughout her pregnancy. She gave birth prematurely, which is common among opiate-addicted mothers. Baby Paddy was underweight and started life in an incubator in the premature baby unit in St James. When I went to see him, his woollen hat bobbled on his tiny head as he twitched from narcotic withdrawals. He tested negative for HIV but there was no great joy in this because we were still uncertain as to how the virus manifested itself. We had linked in with colleagues in health and social services in Edinburgh. From them we learned that some babies born with the virus seemed to shed it and some, who initially tested negative, acquired it. We just had to wait and see. With the benefit of longitudinal studies, it was later shown in the late 1990s that cases of AIDS among the children of intravenous drug users was as low as 2 per cent.

Despite all our procrastination, we easily found a short-term foster home for baby Paddy when the time came for his discharge from hospital. Leah didn't even ask to bring him home and agreed to him being placed in care voluntarily. She asked that he be baptised before being placed. 'Just in case,' she said. Through the hospital chaplain we arranged a small ceremony in the church on the hospital grounds just before we headed off to place Paddy. Leah walked her baby from the ward to the church and we took some photographs of them during the ceremony. The foster parents were provided with liquid medication and tiny syringes to draw, measure and administer it. They were more concerned with having to administer narcotic withdrawal medication than they were about HIV.

Leah's addiction was rampant now. She wasn't looking after herself and the weight was falling off her. One day she opened the door to me in her nighty. It hung from her like it was pegged to a clothesline, filled with nothing but a waft of air. Then she got herself arrested for shoplifting. It was like her HIV diagnosis had washed away any remaining defences and she was now swept along on a torrent of self-destruction. We held a case conference, including staff from community health, the maternity hospital and Jervis Street. The two older girls were in voluntary care and things just drifted along like that. But it was time to take stock. Leah's lifestyle, and now life expectancy, was not good. It was decided to go for a care order in respect of all three children.

She got herself a lawyer, but in truth she didn't put up a fight. In a situation where other parents had spat, punched and cursed, Leah didn't even have a cross word for me. Her solicitor just went through the motions in court, and we got the orders virtually uncontested. It made the paper because the judge commented that the care orders would last until the new millennium. And we all knew that was more than could be said for Leah.

In a move that pleased us all, including Leah, we moved Paddy from his short-term placement to the long-term foster home with his sisters. He was just a few months old when he arrived. They would all be together until they reached eighteen, and beyond that if they chose. As Leah's health declined the children's attachment to the foster carers grew. Often, in long-term placements, the children gradually relate to the foster carer as the parent figure, with the natural parent being gradually relegated to the status of significant other. This phenomenon manifested itself soon after Paddy's arrival. The foster mother was changing his nappy with the sisters looking on. 'Oh look,' one of them said, 'his pee pee is all broken.'

'Never mind', the other said, patting the foster mother on the arm, 'Mammy will fix it.'

Leah, or 'Mammy Leah' as the children began to call her, never did see the millennium. She had become a ghostly impersonation of herself, an urban banshee as life itself evaporated from her. In the end her death wasn't a big punctuating event – she just glided lightly into an eternal sleep.

12

No Fixed Abode

O n 3 October 2017, I watched as over 10,000 people marched on Leinster House to have the housing crisis declared a national emergency. Rising house prices, exorbitant rents and a shortage of public housing has created a new homeless classification – the homeless family. When the problem was confined to social outcasts such as rough sleepers, hostel dwellers and even youth homeless, it was housed on the margins of public thinking. But now it is the political chopping block upon which the electoral axe is poised.

As a child I knew about Forty Coats, even though he was long gone. A notorious street dweller in Dublin city centre, Forty Coats got his name from the layers he wore to insulate himself against the cold. This amused passers-by. Through the generations, others came and went, winning the affection of Dublin's citizenry, once they were colourful and amusing enough to be considered 'characters'. Their depiction as characters was entirely in the eye of the beholder, because the only thing they had going for them was their own particular brand of entertaining insanity. Other, less flamboyant vagrants were seen merely as beggars and pests.

In the early 1970s, like so many twenty-something-year-olds, I joined the Dublin Simon Community as a volunteer to help homeless rough sleepers and street drinkers. The Simon Community was founded in England by Anton Wallich Clifford, a probation officer in Bow Street, London. Through this work he observed that those who needed help the most were the least likely to seek it. Therefore outreach measures, such as a soup run, were developed as a means of bringing help to people in need, rather than needing people to seek help in a centre. Wallich Clifford also observed that human companionship was valued more than food and shelter. Showing that you care was the key, just as Simon of Cyrene had done when he helped Christ carry the cross to Calvary. In 1969, he came to Dublin to speak at UCD, Earlsfort Terrace, about the rootless Irish in London. Arising from this some students organised and formed Dublin Simon later in the same year.

Dublin Simon ran a nightly soup run, a night shelter and a couple of longer-term residential houses. I volunteered one evening per week in the night shelter at Sarsfield Quay. The building was rough and ready, perfectly complimenting the clientele. These were the single homeless, rootless and adrift in the city by day, unclaimed by health and social services because they were disconnected from a catchment-based system, disenfranchised by the State and often disowned by their families. To the general public they were a menace, threatening because of their appearance as much as their behaviour. But in the eyes of the homeless person, they were the overlooked and the stepped over, prone to ridicule and banished from mainstream society.

In 1975, I went to work full-time for a year in Simon's head office at 42 Harcourt Street, one of a number of Georgian buildings demolished to make way for Garda Headquarters. One of three full-time officers, I was responsible for the recruitment of volunteers and their deployment across the projects. Just before I left to go to college to train as a social worker, I opened a letter that was addressed to 'the person in charge'. It encapsulated so charmingly the fragility and innocence of a typical Simon resident that I kept it ever since as a reminder. Here it is, verbatim, except for the writer's real name:

*Mountjoy Prison
10/6/76*

To the person in charge, Please tell Corkie to go to the Skipper and he will find a pair of specks on the book beside the open air fireplace. Failing that tell him to go where I sleep and he should [find] about two pair there and if successful bring what he can as I can't read nothing without them.

I got a month for Drunk and D.H. [disorderly] on 10/6/76 aloud one visit a week. I could do with a smoke matches cig-paper so I Thrust you will Oblige.

I am Kerrie, the fellow that had the black dog.

As this biro is Dodgie I'll say Good Luck.

Here's hoping

Tell him only when <u>Sober</u>

*

The first time I encountered youth homelessness was in 1984, when I transferred from the Social Work Department in Killarney Street to the one in Lord Edward Street on the south-side. Jason's exasperated mother kicked him out because she just couldn't control him. An only child, he was out of school, moped around the falt all day and could be violent to her when challenged. It was all about behaviour – he didn't drink, smoke or take drugs. When I took over the case Jason, aged sixteen, was sleeping in a shed up the road from where he lived. He always had a hammer inside his coat.

The case was one of a number transferred to me by Frank Deasy, who was leaving to develop a career in script-writing. Such is Ireland's parochial nature that Frank and I grew up around the corner from each other and went to the same school. In 1986, he invited me and other social workers from the team to the world premiere of his first movie, *Sometime City*, which screened in the Irish Film Theatre. It was my first and last invite to a world premiere and I still have the card. The movie was a great insight into the workings of the social work team at that time and we had fun putting real-life names to the characters. Frank went on to have a successful career, winning an Emmy for the television series *Prime Suspect*. He was only fifty when he died of liver cancer in 2009, immediately after a liver transplant.

By the time Frank introduced me to Jason, he had already ploughed through the few residential placements that were available. A couple of voluntary organisations existed ostensibly as places for homeless boys, but in reality they would run a mile if they saw one. There was no question of taking someone in an emergency. They liked to have a good look at the young people before accepting them, to make sure they weren't trouble. Neither did they like any semblance of disability, or the over-involvement of families in the placements. For these reasons I once described them in an internal memo as confining their admission criteria to intelligent orphans who were not in a hurry to be placed.

Having exhausted all official placement options, I resorted one evening to booking Jason into a B&B on Gardiner Street. It was a shocking and unprecedented juncture to place a teenager on his own in commercial accommodation. Unfortunately, over the next few years it became the norm for young people who could not be placed in the care system. Imperceptibly, the profile of young people had changed and many had challenging behaviours that mainstream residential facilities didn't want to touch. The problem was, there were only mainstream residential facilities.

At one point I got him into what is now Oberstown Detention Centre in Lusk. On the face of it, it was for 'an assessment' – in reality it was to get him off the street for a while. Oberstown takes in young people who are on remand for or convicted of offences. Often social workers stood accused of criminalising young people in order to secure a placement for them. This is probably a fair accusation. But it wasn't just to secure a placement, it was to obtain a secure placement where the door was locked and the young person would not just walk out when they felt like it.

Jason was back on the street after his assessment and I was back booking him into B&Bs. He seldom lasted more than one night because at best he was noisy and truculent. One morning, after he got kicked out of yet another B&B on Gardiner Street, I seriously thought of taking him on the ferry to Holyhead to recommence the nightly scrounge for a bed over there. He was living hand-to-mouth, so I arranged with the community welfare officer to get him a daily allowance. He was on £5 per day for personal expenses excluding the B&B, which was considerably more that I had at my disposal. God knows what he used it for because he was always hungry, dirty and tired.

In the evenings I often brought him into cafes to buy him a meal. In one such cafe on O'Connell Street, the waitress took pity on him. He had ordered liver and chips. She continued to top up his plate with slices of liver and he continued to eat them. Decades later, I cannot pass that particular emporium without retching. I brought home his clothes to wash. On the days when I couldn't place him, he returned to his shed as I drove to my centrally heated suburban home. I thought of Simon's simple philosophy of shelter and companionship. At one point, on the phone home, I kind of hinted that maybe we could put him up for a while. To give Mary her due, she didn't baulk at the idea. Yet I knew I wasn't a missionary – there had to be boundaries to the relationship and a limit to what I, as a professional social worker, could be expected to do for him.

The Marist Fathers had a go at providing a hostel for unattached teenage boys. I brought Jason to their house on Percy Place. A priest from the posh Catholic University School in Leeson Street was the manager. He ran through a big list of dos and don'ts for Jason. Then he explained to Jason that he wanted to create an atmosphere of study in the house and that he would require Jason to comply with this. 'Any questions?' he chirped when he was done. Jason responded with a question of his own, 'What does comply mean?' When the priest went out to make tea Jason pulled the hammer out from inside his coat and scraped the letter J into the table. 'It's for Jesus', he tittered.

I brought Jason to AnCo, the State training council of the day. The training officer quizzed him on what areas he would like to become skilled in. He said he liked the fish market in the city centre. When asked what the attraction was, Jason replied in apparent sincerity, 'I like messing with dead fish.' The training officer pitched me a business card and said, 'You find a placement – anywhere – and I'll pay for it.'

One evening, Jason was in our offices in Lord Edward Street when I was phoning around B&Bs which hadn't yet heard of him. Dermot McMahon, my senior social worker, was there too. I knew Dermot from Dublin Simon. He was one of the earliest volunteers and co-wrote a book called *A Group Approach to Socially Deprived People*. Jason was fed up. He started to scrape the desk with his hammer. Dermot told him to stop and instinctively grabbed his wrist. Jason exploded. The months of boring days and miserable nights had caught up with him and he went for us with the hammer. By the time Dermot and I could restrain him he had hit me a couple of times on the back, and he also bit my arm. A social worker in the other room called the Gardaí and we held him on the floor until they arrived. They cuffed him, took him off and charged him with assault.

Jason quickly appeared in the Children's Court. I was taken aback to see him arrive shackled to two prison officers. They released him at the door of the court. He was still fuming, and full of hatred towards us. Dermot and I gave evidence, reasoning that he needed to learn the consequences of his actions. His accommodation requirements were ameliorated when he was sentenced to six months in St Patrick's Institution. It was his first conviction. When sentenced he broke free and, dashing to the witness box, hurled the bible at the judge, hitting him on the chest. If he had a heart, the bible would have gone right through.

Making matters worse, Jason shouted at the judge, 'You specky four-eyed bastard.'

'What did he say?' the judge asked.

'I said, you culchie, specky four-eyed bastard.'

The judge dismissed the whole incident with an amused shrug as Jason was cuffed and frog-marched away.

While in St Patrick's, Jason obsessed about what he was going to do to me when he got out. The psychiatrist, whom I knew from my time in the psychiatric service, made a suggestion.

He proposed that I come and visit and, in the controlled environment of the institution, allow Jason to take a few swings at me. This, he theorised, would ventilate his frustration and anger. I wasn't too enamoured with the plan, despite the promise of a room full of prison officers, but I went along with it. On the day I went to see him he was upbeat and cheerful. No one else had been to see him, not even his mother, so I was better than nothing to this deserted teenager.

When he got out he did come gunning for me. I moved to alternative offices – a port-a-cabin in Terenure which froze in winter and baked in summer. Eventually Jason lost interest and we all moved on.

*

In the mid-1980s Jason was an exception but, unfortunately, over the next decade there were many like him who followed down the same cul-de-sac. Teenagers whose behaviour saw them excluded from their families, the school system and, to a large extent, the care system which couldn't cope with them either. Robbie Gilligan, Professor of Social Work and Social Policy in Trinity College Dublin, summarised this crashing through of boundaries into a kind of law: 'out of school, out of home, out of control.' Once the first defence wall went the others became much more vulnerable – hence the importance of schools hanging onto challenging teenagers rather than taking the easy way out. Right through the 1990s, cases were brought before the High Court by campaigning solicitors on behalf of these teenagers to have their right to a care placement upheld. Judge Peter Kelly heard many of these constitutional cases. He directed the State to make adequate provision for such young people and once described the Eastern Health Board as being in 'an administrative torpor' in this regard.

In reality the system was caught on the hop. The residential care system was largely invested in the voluntary system, which was subsidised by the health boards. Most of these services were provided by religious orders who, to a large extent, could pick and choose which children they would take. While more specialist services were being developed for challenging teenagers, the Eastern Health Board resorted to make-shift facilities staffed by security guards and psychiatric nurses doing nixers. Eventually purpose-built special care facilities were constructed at enormous cost to the State. By order of the High Court, teenagers who were beyond the control of mainstream care services could be involuntarily detained for periods prescribed by the court. Of course, locking people up is not a solution in itself. There has to be rehabilitative progress if special care is to be distinguished from prison. It has to be a stepping-stone to something better, not a repository for the unmanageable.

Throughout the 1990s, services for homeless teenagers were developed and improved. In 1992, I was the head social worker for Dublin North West, referred to in those days in functional terms as Community Care Area 6. I got a call from John Doyle, the senior administrator in Community Care. He had just been to a meeting with the Gardaí and Sr Stanislaus Kennedy, the well-known social justice campaigner, where he was under fire because there was no out-of-hours service. Social workers essentially worked nine to five so unattached teenagers had nowhere to turn to at night if they were stuck for a bed. Consequently, many ended up in Garda stations, which improvised as a place of refuge. John asked me what I thought of the idea of setting up an out-of-hours social work service. I told him that would be the icing on the cake, but that we were still scrambling around for the ingredients to bake it. 'Mmm', he said and rang off. The next day he phoned back and told me to do it. He said I could have three staff, and to come back to him with a proposal in a week.

In March 1992, the new out-of-hours service (OHS) went live, covering Dublin, Wicklow and Kildare and I managed this as well as the regular social work team. A single social worker went on duty, each evening and worked through the night. They had at their disposal a small number of ring-fenced placements where they could place people until the following day. Controversially, the young people could only access the service by presenting at a Garda station where the Gardaí would then

Hanged If You Do...

contact the OHS. Very soon the dedicated OHS beds became a coveted resource to the daytime social workers. It meant that if they couldn't manage to place a young person by day, they knew they could go home with a relatively clear conscience by telling the kid to present at the Garda station that night.

The OHS social worker carried a mobile phone – a sexy piece of kit in 1992. They in turn were backed up by a roster of senior social workers who, for a pittance, carried another mobile phone and remained on call through the night and over weekends in their own home. These were the original brick mobiles. On weekends in the supermarket or out walking, I carried it about self-consciously, willing it to silence. Once I had to bring it to a Christmas pantomime with my children, where I pleaded with it not to go off. This was at a time where there were no mute buttons or even ringtone volume control. Was that you on the mobile phone? Oh yes it was! We backup staff only had one mobile phone between us, so it had to be passed on to the next person after each shift, as I had to do one Christmas Day. In the box for the mobile phone was a baby vodka bottle with a label which read, 'In case of emergency, break seal.'

*

When I was appointed Director of Child Care Services in the Eastern Health Board in 1995, one of my responsibilities was services for homeless children. It was a conspicuous political issue at the time, so the Department of Health and Children had eyes on it. Parkview B&B on the North Circular Road was a popular place for social workers to find a bed for hard to place teenagers. The proprietor, for personal reasons, was sympathetic to the youngsters and tolerated behaviour that others would not. My first port of call in the new job was to him. Making him an offer he couldn't refuse, I booked out the whole B&B for a year, exclusively for our use. Then I put in a team of child care workers. It became a valuable new placement option for young people no one else would take. And because it was under our management, we nurtured a philosophy that all were welcome, no matter what.

In an attempt to really get to grips with the problem, we established a Forum on Youth Homelessness in 1999. It brought together all the key players for the voluntary and statutory sectors. It was launched by Frank Fahy TD, Minister of State in the Department of Health and Children. There was an independent chair, Dr Miriam Hederman O'Brien, a distinguished, no-nonsense barrister and academic. Members came from the Department of Health and Children, the Department of Education, the Eastern Health Board, youth services, the Probation Service, and Dublin Corporation. Key players from the voluntary sector included Focus Ireland, the Daughters of Charity and the Arrupe Society in the person of Fr Peter McVerry, the high-profile campaigner and outspoken critic of the statutory sector when it came to homeless services.

In just one year the Forum published a significant report proposing a roadmap in areas such as access to services, care and accommodation, and coordination. It was the first time agreement was reached on defining the problem, quantifying it and reaching agreement on what needed to be done. But before the ink was dry on the page, Peter McVerry was on the radio saying there was no plan for homeless young people. I went on after him, pointing out that we had spent the past year devising one, with him. Peter's passion for the cause is beyond doubt but there were several occasions when we clashed over the airwaves over details and interpretation.

*

When we got into the 2000s, the problem stabilised somewhat as further provision and better preventative services were put in place. There came a time when we looked around cautiously and asked ourselves the question, is it possible that we've done something right? Then the focus shifted to homeless families. So now Simon, the original homeless charity, is described as a housing organisation as well as one for street dwellers. Even Barnardos, the children's charity, has latched onto the cause of homeless families. Youth homelessness has been eclipsed to such an extent that, in 2017, Focus Ireland and the National Youth Council launched a campaign to highlight Ireland's 'Hidden Homeless'. They pointed out that there was a huge increase in homelessness among young people between eighteen and twenty-four years.

When it comes to quantifying the problem, there is much counting of apples and oranges. The Department of Housing, Planning and Local Government counts state-funded emergency accommodation. The Reception and Integration Agency counts asylum seekers in direct provision. The Child and Family Agency counts subjects of domestic violence in residential services. And the Dublin Regional Homeless Executive does a biannual survey of rough sleepers. A virtual homeless industry has emerged, with each sector carving out its own market. It is a far cry from the days when Anton Wallich Clifford gave a lot of himself, as well as food and shelter, to rootless rough sleepers in London.

Meanwhile, I was listening to the radio news a few years back. There was a report that Jason was sentenced to Mountjoy for drug offences. The reason it got airtime was because he told the judge he was glad to be going to prison. He said it was a lot safer for him in the Joy than it was out on the street where he was wanted by some very dangerous people. He was described as being of no fixed abode.

13

Sleeping Soundly in Our Beds

hen I was growing up we could hear the Artane Boys' Band rehearsing from our back garden. Undoubtedly the most illustrious act to come out of Artane, it was formed under the auspices of the Artane Industrial School. The band became an integral part of GAA fixtures and was the public face of the school, playing before bishops, presidents and taoisigh at all major GAA events. But behind this facade it was a different tune.

The Christian Brothers opened Artane in 1870 to provide disadvantaged children with education and industrial training. In the year of my birth, 1953, there were almost 700 boys in residence. It was also the year in which the first toilets were installed, replacing the previous slop bucket regime. At home we were told that Artane was where the bold boys were sent. My mother would threaten me with it in moments of exasperation. Although her heart wasn't really in it, my worst fear was that she might one day act upon the ultimatum.

In reality, the vast majority of the boys were committed there because of parental shortcomings or outright destitution. Occasionally we would pass Artane while out walking and see them plodding in rows from the main building to the front gate

Hanged If You Do...

that adjoined the high walls, then back again. They walked in tattered rows, three abreast, patrolled by Christian Brothers. The driveway itself had a rural feel to it, skirted by white railings and fields beyond where daffodils grew in springtime. We observed them with passing curiosity as one might gaze upon cattle in a pastural scene.

There were always stories of cruelty emanating from the school but conclusive evidence emerged when the Commission to Inquire into Child Abuse reported in 2009. In an Orwellian twist, the adults who were there to protect the children were in fact the main source of danger. The boys lived in the certain knowledge that they would be beaten and in justifiable fear that they might be sexually abused. The Brothers had plenty of money to adequately provide for them, but they didn't. The children wore patched and dirty clothes and their beds were equally miserable and cold. At mealtimes all the food was piled on long tables for them to scavenge, like the pigs which got the slops after them.

While my sister and I cozied up at home to read children's versions of the Dickens' classics, *Oliver Twist* was actually living up the road, partitioned by the institutional walls which kept us well insulated from them.

The Commission to Inquire into Child Abuse examined all the institutions providing residential care, the very names of which sent shivers down the spine of generations – Artane, Letterfrack, Daingean, Goldenbridge. After years of probing, the Commission concluded that physical and sexual abuse was endemic in the institutions. Unreasonable and oppressive physical punishment was the norm, where a climate of fear was nurtured and maintained. The deferential attitude of inspectors to the religious congregations enabled cruel regimes to flourish. The system of capitation grants led to institutional managers demanding more committals allowing congregations to prosper while the children went without. They suffered emotional abuse through the complete absence of empathy from staff and the systematic application of ridicule, humiliation and degradation.

Children were constantly told that they were worthless. But here's the thing, they were. They were not just a sub-class, they were considered to be a sub-species. No contemporary observer, or society at large, saw them as equal. If they were equal, they would not have been treated with such abomination. There was no obligation on their carers to nurture or empathise – it was sufficient to maintain the children as one might a caged animal.

To understand how such cruelty could be willingly inflected on vulnerable people, it is necessary to view events through the value system which prevailed at the time, and not with the myopic wisdom of hindsight. In Ireland, we have an outstanding record of retrospective judgement in the area of child care. Through a contemporary prism we judge the shortcomings of previous generations, blind to the fact that future generations will judge us in a similar manner. The current system of warehousing asylum seekers, which we as a society are tolerating, is our Artane. When the children who are suffering under it reach majority and sue the State, as they will, a Commission will be established to tell us what we already knew, but didn't care enough to stop.

*

Following the establishment of the Free State Government in 1922, the first Dáil set about dismantling the British workhouse system, which was seen as inefficient as well as degrading. The establishment of county homes and hospitals ensured the separation of the old and the sick from paupers, who were on the lowest rung of that caste system. A nineteenth-century attitude lingered whereby the destitute were considered to be victims of their own perversity. Consequently, no love was lost on the occupants of the State's orphanages, industrial schools, reformatories, Magdalen laundries, and mother and baby homes.

As I write, the Government has just approved a plan for the forensic excavation and recovery of children's remains from a sewer on the grounds of the mother and baby home in Tuam, run by the Bon Secour Sisters since 1925. Like all similar institutions, the Government of the day was content to allow religious orders shoulder the responsibility for such services, in the absence of any statutory service provision. But as recipients of Government grant aid, the religious congregations were agents of the State, providing services on its behalf. State inspection systems were in place which either condoned the contemporary standards or deferred to the religious who perched on a pedestal of respectability where society had placed them. In this way our institutions operated outside mainstream society, on the fringes of our towns or behind high walls where ordinary citizens did not have to be bothered by them. With this insight, I look back now at the boys in the industrial school in Artane who seldom received my interest and never received my sympathy.

*

By the time I started in social work, the big institutions were pretty much gone. While the buildings lived on, efforts were made to create spaces within them that were conducive to the running of a modern children's home. They were like an old mansion that had been converted into apartments. The first time I visited Goldenbridge in Inchicore it was like that – a big imposing building where, deep inside, small numbers of children rattled about like church mice in a cathedral. In its heyday, Goldenbridge catered for 150 girls. By the 1980s, it was dealing with boys and girls in groups no bigger than nine or ten. However, like several other religious orders providing residential care, the sisters at Goldenbridge moved the operation out of the institutional building entirely. In a far corner of their extensive grounds, butting up against the Grand Canal, they built two brand new units. These were detached houses, purpose-built and of a high standard of specification and design.

The reputation of Goldenbridge began to unravel in 1996 when an RTE documentary, *Dear Daughter*, made serious allegations of abuse. This was confirmed when the Commission to

Inquire into Child Abuse reported in 2009. It found that there was a cruel regime of excessive physical punishment. Children were humiliated and belittled in a system that was devoid of any kindness. The Commission also found that children were subjected to the daily drudgery of rosary-bead-making and other forms of child labour. The Sisters of Mercy showed little actual mercy to the children in their care.

In my day, things had moved on and the children's home was run by lay and largely qualified staff. But the resident manager was a nun who was still very much in charge. I once sought to place a child in Goldenbridge when the managing sister asked me, 'Well, if she's bold will you take her back?' This typified a regime which prevailed in the 1980s and well into the 1990s. Children's homes were almost exclusively run by religious or voluntary organisations who had virtual control over which children were admitted or discharged. The criteria for either could be changed without a by-your-leave to the social workers who made the placements, or the health board which paid for them. The needs of the children requiring placement were secondary to the interests of the regime. Therefore, compliant and high-achieving children had better prospects of being placed than those with attitude or limited ability. The only thing that passed for any semblance of inspection was an annual visit from a health board administrator to the nun in charge. This would primarily involve cups of tea in the parlour followed by a discreet and slightly embarrassed discussion about money.

*

While most of the newer children's homes were single houses, or two houses beside each other, Madonna House was different. It originally opened in 1955 at the request of Dr J.C. McQuaid, the Catholic archbishop of Dublin, catering for the very young children of mothers who were sick at home or in hospital. Then it moved to Blackrock in 1971 where a new 'children's village' was built. It comprised of five residential units, a pre-school, school, administrative block, central kitchen and dining block, and a playground. There was nothing else like it. In a way that was a good thing because in essence, Madonna House was an institution, just spread out over modern single-storey units, instead of upwards in institutional stone. The little residents lived in 'family groups' of up to twelve children from newborns to ten years of age. They had their breakfast and lunch in their individual units, but they were marched over to the kitchen/dining block in the evening for dinner, like miniature internees.

Madonna House had one great asset – it accepted children on an unplanned and emergency basis. This was a massive and highly treasured resource to social workers who needed a placement in a hurry and, as such, it took in hundreds of children each year. It was prepared to take on children blindly with minimal information from social workers, while other children's homes scrutinised with the exacting eye of a horse dealer. The first time I visited Madonna House was with a boy of about four years of age requiring an emergency placement. His mother had literally placed him on my desk like a parcel and marched out of the office. That was her way of telling me she couldn't cope without getting the whole lecture on the best interest of the child.

Driving onto the campus at Madonna House with the little boy in the back, I was gobsmacked at the architectural splendour of the children's village. All it lacked was holiday redcoats. I went to the administrative block to do the paperwork. The manager swayed back and forth in his swivel chair, behind a desk as big as a dance floor, as he spoke into a telephone apparatus from the future. 'Sisters of Charity?' I mused – if this is poverty I want to see chastity.

In 1993, the Eastern Health Board reported to the Minister of Health that it was investigating allegations of child sexual abuse and other misconduct against a number of staff in Madonna House. The Gardaí were also involved, resulting in the conviction and imprisonment of a staff member. Inevitably an inquiry followed. It was chaired by Fred Donohue, the recently retired supremo of all the Eastern Health Board's community-based health and social services. While Fred perfected the image of a somewhat gawkish countryman, lurking beneath the unpolished exterior was a sharp and cunning mind that was usually two steps ahead of his adversaries. And he had a repertoire of stories for every occasion with which he used to beguile all-comers. I was with him once while he greeted a delegation from Focus Ireland led by Sr Stanislaus Kennedy. Stan was accompanied by a high-powered group of influences, including some celebrities – the type who wear sunglasses indoors. As she made her pitch for more funding Fred countered with, 'Ah now, don't be talking to me about money until we have a sup of tay,' as he distracted the room with one of his anecdotes. Once I heard him say, before meeting a group of applicants, 'Give them plenty of sweet talk, but no money.'

By the time the inquiry report was issued, Madonna House was history. In 1994, the Sisters of Charity announced their intention to close Madonna House and did so the following year. But something sinister had happened there, which undermined its standing and there was no outlet for us social workers to ventilate this. I gave evidence to the inquiry team, if that is not too grandiose a description of the process, but it didn't feel like closure. It felt like those in charge, whom we knew and trusted, had slipped away like a fox into a thicket.

In advance of the closure, arrangements were made to decant all the children to other centres. The budget from Madonna House was used to buy and staff new houses in areas of greatest need. There had always been a high ratio of children's homes in the Blackrock area. This related more to the addresses of original charitable benefactors than it did to the localities from which the children were coming. I was working in the north-west of Dublin and our area got one of the new children's homes. Glenview was a detached bungalow on the outskirts of Blanchardstown, where it was well accepted by neighbours and the community. The new staff were employed directly by the health board and I became their line manager.

*

By the mid-1990s religious and voluntary organisations were getting out of residential care in large numbers, so the health

Hanged If You Do...

board was taking over more and more homes and getting involved in direct provision. At one stage, we were negotiating with two religious orders at the same time. Both had a history of providing institutional care but had constructed purpose-built children's homes on their grounds. Now they wanted the health board to take over the operation. This required human resource and estate management, as well as child care management. The first objective was to ensure a smooth transfer of management so that the children would hardly notice the difference in their daily lives. The next was the transfer of staff from a voluntary to a statutory organisation, with all the red tape and industrial relations which that entailed. Then there was the transfer of property, and that was by far the most intriguing. One religious order handed their property, worth millions, over to the State for nothing. The other order demanded, and got, top dollar for it.

From the 1980s onward, foster care was rapidly replacing residential care as the primary type of care provision. In the 1960s, there were 3,000 children in residential care and by 2017 there were just 300. Now 95 per cent of children in care are fostered. Residential care has become a more specialised resource, catering for children with significant behavioural difficulties, sibling groups and homeless teenagers. This makes for a much more diverse constituency with thousands of individual children living in regular families across the country, all of whom have to be supervised and supported. Reflecting on this metamorphosis, Fred Donohue, chair of the Madonna House Inquiry, commented tongue-in-cheek, but with just a hint of nostalgia, 'God be with the days when there was a thousand children in Artane and we could all sleep soundly in our beds.'

14

Someone Else's Child

I was looking at the 1911 Census with an elderly relative. Two children with a different surname were listed as residing in his house. When I asked who the children were he said, matter-of-factly, 'They were someone else's from up the road.' The other family had too many young mouths to feed, so his family took them in. It reminded me of Olive Stevenson's influential book from the 1970s, *Someone Else's Child,* written to assist foster parents in raising a child who is not their own.

There is a long tradition of fostering in Ireland going back to the Brehon Laws, which did not confine the concept of family to the nuclear version. It facilitated the shared rearing of children across families and the wider community. Neither was it confined to orphans and strays. It commonly applied to children in large families where the number of children simply outgrew the household space available to physically contain them. Consequently, they were boarded out with families that had the space to accommodate them.

The introduction of the British Poor Law system to Ireland in 1838 relied upon the workhouse as a last resort for paupers, including children. No outdoor relief was provided, thereby forcing those requiring relief to come inside for it. And only the most desperate would subject themselves to the harsh regime of the workhouse. About thirty years after the introduction of the Poor Law, boarding out was introduced as an alternative to children having to enter the workhouse. In 1923, the Irish Government began to dismantle the harsh British system. It placed the administration of relief under Boards of Assistance, which operated at county level. Then the Health Act 1953, which established the health boards, provided for the care of children by boarding them out with families or otherwise to place them in an approved school.

Under the Health Act, a contractual arrangement was provided for between health boards and foster parents. They would receive a maintenance allowance to cover the child's food, clothing and general upkeep. Regulations followed in 1954 stipulating that foster care should be the first option for a child. It also stipulated that foster carers should be assessed for their suitability, then matched appropriately with a child. Periodic inspections of the foster home were required. The allowance to foster carers applied until the child reached sixteen years or was otherwise engaged in full-time education or training.

When I started in the late 1970s, we were still operating under the 1954 regulations. We were creative in our interpretation of what constituted full-time education or training. Even then, we could hardly cast a child out just because he or she turned sixteen. For assessing foster parents and matching suitable families to children, we relied on standards set by the British Association of Adoption and Fostering (BAAF). This was a high standard. A placement committee, comprising senior administrators and very experienced professionals, oversaw the approvals of foster families and the matching of children. But even then there were loopholes through which the system could be navigated. Short-term placements could be made without the approval of the placement committee. Cunning social workers knew that if they found a family they considered suitable, placed the child short-term and left him there, there wasn't a lot the placement committee could do when the arrangement was eventually brought to its notice. The child would have already bonded with the short-term family, so a transfer of placement would be detrimental. In such circumstances, the placement committee could only approve the arrangement as a long-term placement.

At the end of the 1960s there were around 3,000 children in residential care. Nowadays there are about 350, representing just 8 per cent of the total care population. The gradual shift from residential to foster care was not the subject of some master plan drawn up by Government or the product of a grand internal health board committee. As is often the case in social work, it was just an imperceptible evolution of practice where collective knowledge and continuous learning led us to better ways of doing things for children. By that time too, the religious congregations and voluntary organisations, who until then monopolised residential care, had started to pull out. Another influential factor was the establishment of the Irish Foster Care Association (IFCA), which has been a force of good ever since. It had a humble beginning in 1981, working out of the spare bedroom of one of its earliest members, Pat Whelan. As well as representing the interest of foster careers, the IFCA also been a major contributor to policy and practice development, here in Ireland and internationally through the extensive networks it developed. Throughout all this, Pat Whelan was a key player in the IFCA – a voice of reason as well as experience, she had the ear of successive Government ministers. Such was the scale of her contribution that, when she died in 2007 a void was created, not only in Ireland but in foster care circles across the world.

*

Thanks largely to the innovative thinking of my boss, Ciarán Roche, we were placing children with relatives before relative foster care had a name. We figured out the basics – it was much less traumatic for a child to be placed with someone they knew than with a stranger. If a child had to come into care, Ciarán had us enquire as to whether any relatives might be in a position to care for the child before we looked further afield. It was a no-brainer in retrospect, but good ideas are often simple.

One of the first relative placements I was involved with concerned two sisters who had become orphaned by the ages of nine and ten. They were living in Wales with both parents, who were married, working and settled. Then the mother developed a chronic illness which eventually killed her. The father brought the children back to Ireland. Then he became unwell. The children's maternal uncle and his wife cared for the girls full-time for a while. When the time came for the girls to return to their father, the uncle and aunt didn't want to let them go. It ended up in court, where a direction was made for the girls to be returned to their father. When he arrived to collect them a row broke out. Push turned to shove and, in an horrific and unintentional turn of events, the father fell, incurring a serious spinal injury. He was hospitalised for only a short time when he died of respiratory complications.

The girls were moved to the neutral care of their maternal aunt and settled well there, despite the trauma. Their uncle was a frequent visitor, spending a lot of time with them. After several months in the placement I got call from the aunt who wanted them out straight away. She was very distressed but wouldn't say why. The senior social worker and I held a meeting in the house. The aunt could give no coherent reason but was adamant that the girls had to go. We were baffled. We ended up recruiting a non-relative family for the girls and, eventually, they settled well. Years later the girls disclosed that their uncle was sexually abusing them on his visits to them in his sister's house. That was what the sister had discovered. She had probably caught him in the act but couldn't bring herself to tell us. And we were so ignorant of sexual abuse back then that the possibility never even crossed out minds.

New regulations, which issued in 1995, created a strong mandate for the provision of relative foster care. It defined a relative very broadly as anyone who knew the child or who had acted in *loco parentis*. Therefore, it didn't have to be a blood relative and the next-door neighbour could become a relative career. The regulations also allowed for a child to be placed with a relative in an emergency with only minimal checks being made on the receiving family. The rule was, that a full assessment should be carried out after the crisis and within a specified period of time. Of course, once the child was placed, it was easy for the social worker to put the assessment on the long finger, moving on to the next crisis. In this way, many assessments were left incomplete, technically leaving the children in unapproved placements.

Around this time the Department of Health and Children had enlisted the help of Mike Dolan, the Chief Social Worker for New Zealand. Frank Fahy TD was the Minister of State, a pragmatic man who came up with some whacky ideas and proposals which kept his officials on their toes. Mike advised the Minister and the Department on what worked well in New Zealand. They promoted a system of family welfare conferencing, which brought together the key players within families to troubleshoot the particular difficulties which brought the family to the attention of social workers in the first place. It was a strengths-based approach which built on the positive contributions of family members had to offer. In that way grandparents, for example, might offer to be the primary carer if the parents were not managing. They would then be paid an allowance as part of a family welfare plan agreed between social services and the extended family. The children would not have to come into care, but a relative would receive State subsidy to do the minding.

Somewhere along the line the New Zealand message got lost in translation. The system that transpired in Ireland was one where a child had to be received into State care before a relative could be paid, even though we did introduce the family welfare conferencing element of the New Zealand model. The inevitable upshot of this was that many children who didn't need to be in care were admitted anyway by social workers simply as a method of income maintenance. It is a grave matter to place a child in care and it should only be done in accordance with the legal requirement to protect children from harm. Many of the relative placements under this Irish solution never needed that level of protection – it was just that the families needed some additional financial support.

At first, relative carers were paid a lower rate of allowance than non-relative foster carers. There would be some logic in this if the children were not in care. Even then, there is an argument that relative and stranger foster care are two different things entirely, the latter being more complex. In the late 1990s, many relative carers were agitating for 'equal pay'. I was at a gathering when this issue was passionately raised by a few relative carers. Without as much as a by-your-leave to the Department, Fahy announced from the top table that he was going to increase the allowance to relative carers. Whether he did it as a calculated act or a kneejerk reaction only he can say.

*

There are currently about 4,000 children living in non-relative foster families in Ireland. Many of these become part of the family with lifelong ties. But there are never enough families to meet the demand. It is a natural resource that has never been fully harvested. The difficulty is that child protection takes precedence for social work attention, so that only a small percentage of social work time is taken up with recruiting and maintaining foster homes. It is akin to the trolly crisis in hospitals, where a complex capacity issue manifests itself at the front door in A&E.

For this reason, in the boom time of the early 2000s, private providers became a seductive alternative to growing your own foster families. They came over from the UK, offering to take the pain out of recruitment by providing off-the-shelf recruited and trained families to the statutory sector, which could then focus more exclusively on the core activity of child protection. I was never a supporter of private foster care for two reasons. Firstly, the taxpayer had to fork out four times more than the allowance paid to homegrown foster families. Secondly, I had a respect for the voluntary tradition of foster care provision in Ireland which served us so well across the centuries and was the envy of most countries, even those with well-developed foster care systems.

Like King Canute, I watched as a rising tide of privately recruited families flooded in. It was such a lazy option and a squandering of public funds. Ironically, the financial crash in the mid-1990s provided a further boost to private provision. A moratorium was placed on the recruitment of social workers in 2009 so, robbing Peter to pay Paul, public funds were expended to enable private providers recruit and maintain foster families, instead of the statutory sector. However, in more recent times, increased emphasis on value for money from commissioned services has meant that private provision does not now exceed 10 per cent of the total foster care provision.

The introduction of the Adoption (Amendment) Act 2017 enables foster parents to apply to adopt a child who is left in their care for more than eighteen months in certain circumstances. It is now the right of any child to be adopted, where even married parents may consent to the placement of their child for adoption. Also, where the parents of a child, married or not, failed in their duty to the child, an application can be made to have that child adopted. The fostering task will have to change to allow for the possibility that, if a child is not likely to return home within a reasonable period, they may become eligible for adoption. Unfortunately, to date social workers have been slow at copping on to these new legislative provisions. There is still little evidence to show that the care planning and review process is systematically identifying children in care who could benefit from the permanency of adoption.

National Standards for Foster Care were introduced in 2003 and the Health Information and Quality Authority (HIQA) monitors foster care against these standards. HIQA persistently finds that services are crisis-led rather than delivered in a planned manner. It should not come entirely out of the blue to HIQA that a crisis intervention service does not have the luxury of working entirely to an unalterable script, but must roll with the punches of daily demands. Child protection is the business of risk management. Risks have not only to be identified, as

HIQA does so well, but they often have to be taken if services are not to be completely stifled by regulatory inertia.

HIQA also regularly finds that there are shortcomings in the timely recruitment of relative carers. This has led to many 'shock horror' headlines that children are left in unapproved families where assessments remain incomplete. This, strictly speaking, is true. But a child, for example, who is placed with his maternal aunt because his mother is unable to look after him can hardly be described as being at risk. Indeed, was it ever necessary for him to be placed in care in the first place? Referring back to the New Zealand model, this child could have benefited from remaining outside the care system, without all the bells and whistles of State monitoring and inspection, by simply giving his aunt some money to look after him.

Returning to my elderly relative's family – they were never assessed when they opened their door to neighbours in need. Have these traditional Irish values of informal care become the baby that has been thrown out with the bath water?

15

Adopting the Right Attitude

*I*n the early 1990s, a man came into my office and more or less offered me a blank cheque. It wasn't a bribe – but he had money, I had something he desperately wanted, and he was prepared to pay a lot for it. Following the fall of the Iron Curtain and all the political upheaval in Eastern Europe towards the end of the 1980s, the plight of abandoned children in appalling institutions found its way onto our television screens. It made uncomfortable viewing and Irish people wanted to do something about it. With the decline in the availability of Irish children for adoption, childless individuals and couples who could afford it looked to Eastern Europe as a means of rescue by adoption. The man who came to see me wanted my help to do this.

At first, couples were going to institutions in Romania and elsewhere to adopt these deserted, and often institutionalised, children. But they were bringing them back to a legal limbo because there was as yet no legislation governing the adoption of foreign children in Ireland. There was little or no vetting of prospective adopters either and rumours abounded of money changing hands between would-be parents and those doing the mediating. The man who came to see me wanted me to do a report supporting him and his wife as suitable to adopt, that could then be presented to the authorities abroad. I couldn't help him because I had my hands full managing a social work team in Dublin. But plenty of people were doing this work as nixers, and not always to a high standard. I had seen some of their reports – a couple of pages outlining the bare details of income, health and a few lines on their capacity to parent.

Then, when the Foreign Adoption Act 1991 was commenced, it required prospective adopters to be the subjects of a home study assessment report, addressing their eligibility and suitability to become adoptive parents. This was to be completed by health boards or registered adoption societies and then passed on to the Adoption Board to make the ultimate declaration of their suitability. The Act also provided for the establishment of a Register of Foreign Adoption to be held by the Adoption Board, so the State would have oversight of these adoptions.

Just as the provisions of the Act were beginning to kick in, in 1995, I was appointed co-director of Child and Family Services in the Eastern Health Board, with responsibility for adoption services. The new legislation had a couple of significant elements that assisted prospective adopters. The first was that they were entitled in law to an assessment. Coming from a background in child protection, where I was more familiar with imposing a service on people who actively resisted it, this was a culture shock. I was now faced with new cohort of service users who not only wanted a service but demanded one.

The second element was that the legislation required health boards to undertake these assessments 'as soon as practicable'. This was understandably interpreted by adoption applicants as 'without delay' whereas I, constrained by scarce resources, interpreted it as 'as soon as possible.' The ever-increasing demand resulted in an ever-increasing waiting list for assessment. As all applicants were entitled to an assessment no one, no matter how obviously unsuited, could be screened out at the application stage. And, unlike domestic adoption, no upper age limit could be imposed. In this way some very sick and relatively old people had to be assessed even though they hadn't a chance of being considered suitable to adopt.

Applicants formed representative groups and I met them regularly. They took an actuarial approach to monitoring waiting lists, calibrating every little detail to the weight of a mustard seed. Our meetings were often contentious, as we squabbled over everything except the welfare of children. From a quality assurance perspective, I respected people's right to challenge, but there was a limit to the number of social workers we could allocate to foreign adoption. I didn't expect the representative groups to be concerned with our other statutory responsibilities, but child protection had to remain a top priority for us.

We argued about process – resource allocation, waiting times, the duration of the assessment – with little attention to people, young or old. Back then, my life experience couldn't shine a light into the cavernous hole in theirs. After some brutal meetings, I brushed off their anger and frustration as I drove home to my young family and they drove home to an empty house. I hadn't yet come to understand that bereavement can include the loss of someone you never actually had.

The rights-based approach adopted by applicants created a mindset among many that they were not only entitled to an assessment, but to a child as well. The representative groups vigorously lobbied their politicians and made effective use of the media, where this concept of entitlement found a friend. What minister or broadcaster would not support a respectable, well-off, childless person who wanted to share their home with a deprived child languishing in a foreign institution? The issue of respectable, not so well-off, childless people who could not afford to adopt a foreign child went unexplored.

We social workers were programmed to put the child at the centre – so the task for us was to match families to the needs of children, not the other way around. The Hague Convention on the Protection of Children and Co-operation in Respect of International Adoption (1993) was an international treaty created to ensure that the child adoption only took place in the best interest of children. When it was introduced, children's rights were protected through international law prohibiting the abduction, sale or trafficking of children. While Ireland signed up to Hague in 1993, it was not ratified until 2009 and only incorporated into legislation in 2010.

A common accusation made by lobbyists was that social workers were anti-foreign-adoption. There certainly was a counter-balancing debate that more could have been done to support children and families in their own countries. For instance, Ireland already had a good reputation for supporting famine relief, yet there was no great clammer to adopt the deserted or orphaned children from African countries. From its establishment in 1991 to the end of 2019, the Register of Foreign Adoption shows that while over 1,600 children were adopted from Russia and over 800 from Romania, only 316 children were adopted from the entire African continent over the same period.

The social workers who worked in foreign adoption opted to do so as a chosen career path. For this reason, I never accepted the argument that they were biased against it. From a management perspective it seemed important to avoid wedging social workers into specialisms where they didn't want to be. The social workers who worked on that team wanted the best for children and families alike. I too was singled out by protagonists as having 'an attitude' when it came to foreign adoption, but in truth I didn't. It had been drilled into me long before that my job as a manager was to fulfil the duties set out in legislation. 'Like' didn't enter the equation. No one likes entering someone's home with a court order and removing their children, but sometimes it had to be done. By contrast, facilitating people to become adoptive parents was on the happy side of the spectrum and actually a very fulfilling experience.

In domestic adoption (the adoption of Irish children in Ireland), I occasionally had the great pleasure of making that phone call to adoptive parents telling them that a baby was on the way. I heard the news land with a thump as the person on the other end tried to sound composed – followed by consternation, subdued panic and tears of joy. Friends of mine had just ripped out their kitchen, rendering their home a building site, on the very day the call came from an adoption society. But they didn't trouble the caller with news of their upgrade.

New adoptive parents manage, just like those being handed a human being at the exit door of a maternity hospital.

A big difference between domestic and foreign adoption is that in the former we knew the child to be adopted, and their circumstances, as well as the adoptive family, and we made the match based on that knowledge. But in foreign adoption the child is an abstract thing, a hologram that never materialises during the assessment process. Irish social workers never see the child until after he or she arrives in the country. To that extent the process is less personal and more one-sided than domestic adoption.

As well as being criticised for delays in undertaking assessments, we were also lambasted for how the assessments were conducted once they were commenced. There was no yardstick to guide this work. The legislation was introduced requiring it to be done, but no national guidance or procedure accompanied it. It wasn't a complete shot in the dark because domestic adoption procedures were evolving since legislation was first introduced in 1952. Nevertheless, we took considerable flak from those who suggested we were vindictively installing roadblocks and that we were making it up as we went along. There was criticism in the media regarding perceived intrusive questioning, snooping and snide remarks by social workers about pensioners petitioning for children. I went on various television and radio programmes – but arguing about putting children first was just seen as more bureaucratic bungling. So long as influential people pulled political levers on this emotive issue, we were never going to get ministerial cover. We were in a PR pit without a ladder and, as the media gorged on the story, trust between applicants and social workers starved.

In 1999, I wrote a letter to the national newspapers inviting any adoption applicant who wished to make a complaint to contact me directly. Only five did, not because we were great but because people whose assessment had started didn't want to rock the boat. We commissioned Norah Gibbons, then a senior manager in Barnardos, to review the complaints. She confirmed that the degree of mistrust and suspicion felt by applicants was not conducive to them coming forward with grievances or complaints. She also found that one social worker in particular took longer than average to complete assessments and undertook more visits to applicants than other social workers.

Also in 1999, the Department of Health and Children published a report on standardising inter-country adoption assessments, which it had commissioned the Department of Social Policy and Social Work in UCD to undertake. Not surprisingly, the report highlighted lack of standards or guidance, which led to significant variation in the way assessments were being done, and it didn't spare the Adoption Board or the Department Health and Children in this regard. The report made recommendations for a standardised framework for conducting assessments. I was a member of the task force established to devise the framework and this was published in 2000. At last, a roadmap was agreed upon which provided clear expectations for social workers and applicants alike. By this time, the term 'inter-country adoption' had replaced the colder title of 'foreign adoption'.

From the introduction of legislation in 1991 to the end of 2019, over 8,000 inter-country adoptions have been effected. In a complete inversion of the status quo, Ireland has flipped from being a sending country to being a receiving country. From the 1940s through the 1960s, Ireland engaged in the practice of exporting children for the purposes of adoption. In his renowned book, *Banished Babies* (1997), Mike Milotte describes how 'illegitimate children', born in mother and baby homes, were sent by the nuns who ran them to American families for adoption. It is widely accepted that the practice thrived because it was approved by the Catholic Church, administered by the nuns and facilitated by the civil service. According to Milotte, as many as 2,400 children were sent to the USA between the 1940s and 1970 to meet a demand for children from a white gene pool. What might have happened to those children if they stayed in Ireland is another story.

Now the USA is one of the top ten sending countries to meet the demand for adopted children in Ireland. There has been no hoo-ha about this importation – not so much as a raised eyebrow from the lobbyists and representative groups who have had a lot to say about exportation. It may yet be the case that children adopted from abroad will, in later life, question why it was considered necessary or appropriate for them to leave the country of their birth. While such inquisition would be understandable, they will at least have been assured of protection from the Hague Convention, which was not available to the Irish children traveling in the opposite direction.

These days, inter-country adoption no longer causes a stir and about 300 such adoptions are recognised each year. The heyday for adoption was in the 1960s and 1970s, when upwards of 1,000 adoption orders were made each year. The most common form of domestic adoption now is step-parent adoption where, typically, the mother has married a man who is not the birth father but whom the family wants to have as an equal legal parent. For the past five years or so, I have been a board member of the Adoption Authority of Ireland, where it has been a great pleasure to sit through dozens of ceremonies at which adoption orders are finalised. After a career involving a multitude of enforced separations, the joyful union which each adoption represents has not been diminished by repetition. Each child is wanted, each parent is capable and each family is happy.

16

The Incalculable Benefit of Hindsight

*T*he Kilkenny Incest Investigation Report, published in 1993, was the first non-statutory inquiry into failings in the child care system in Ireland. It was commissioned by the South Eastern Health Board on the instruction of the Minister for Health, Brendan Howlin. Concern arose following the sentencing of a man to prison following convictions for rape, incest and assault. During the trial, it emerged that the victim, the man's daughter, had been in contact with health and social services for years without them being sufficiently effective to make the abuse stop. Media reports of the trial fuelled public concern, which led to the political decision to hold an inquiry.

At the beginning of its report, the authors said they were conscious that in conducting their investigation they had the incalculable benefit of hindsight. It struck me at the time that this was a magnanimous observation for the investigation team to make from the outset. And it had no bearing on the justifiable criticisms that inevitably followed in their report. While the wisdom of hindsight is a well-worn phrase, it was the first time I had heard the concept applied to my line of work. It is so much easier to retrospectively analyse what actually went wrong than it is to prospectively assess what might go wrong.

Four other major non-statutory inquiries followed Kilkenny between 1993 and 2010 – Kelly Fitzgerald (1995), the West of Ireland Farmer (1998), Monageer (2009) and the Roscommon Child Care Case (2010). I was a member of the inquiry teams for two of them.

*

In late February 1995, I was the head social worker for Dublin North West in the Eastern Health Board region. The West of Ireland Farmer case was all over the media. Joseph McColgan, from Sligo, had just been sentenced to twelve years for the brutal physical and sexual assault of his children over many years. Days after the trial ended, I got a call from the programme manager in the Western Heath Board inviting me to become a member of an inquiry team, which his chief executive had decided to establish. He had already checked me out with my programme manager, P.J. Fitzpatrick. I was flattered and accepted without hesitation. The other members of the inquiry team were Dr Sheila Ryan and Michael Bruton. Sheila was the programme manager with the North Eastern Health Board and had been a member of the Kilkenny Incest Investigation team. Michael was a management consultant, former social worker and former programme manager with the Western Health Board.

Joseph McColgan terrorised, raped and savagely assaulted his children between 1976 and 1993. His wife too had been beaten into submission and silence. All the while he was a 'street angel', holding himself out to be a respected member of the community. I have come across a lot of dangerous people over the years, but this man stands out as one of the most pernicious of them all. The frequency and the level of depravity McColgan inflicted on his children still makes me shudder when I recall what he did, so unimpeded for so long. The torture included food deprivation, whipping, beating and perverted sexual acts committed with relentless frequency.

We were to inquire into the health board's involvement in the case and to assess its response in the context of the circumstances that prevailed at the time, and also to assess the likely contemporary level of response. As we got started, I usually set off for Sligo after a day's work in Dublin, with the setting sun in my eyes as I drove west. We spent many long days at our base in Sligo General Hospital and many overnights in the Sligo Park Hotel. While we had no powers to compel people to attend, current and retired professionals willingly participated.

We met the four eldest children, by then adults, together with their solicitor and their partners. They were so obviously damaged by their experience, but their testimony was as dignified as it was graphic. It struck me how close they appeared to each other, bound together like hostages in circumstances no one else can fully appreciate. They even managed to find humour, tittering occasionally between themselves as they recalled some small incident or event. When the children left the room the three of us on the inquiry team, although well-seasoned, were nevertheless greatly affected by what we had just heard. In order to witness their experience, if only fleetingly, we had to drink from the poisoned stream of their childhood.

Our report concluded that legal options to protect the children were not sufficiently explored. While there was awareness of non-accidental injury, there appeared to be an ignorance of or incredulity at the existence of sexual abuse in some quarters. This led to indicators not being picked up or acted upon. There was also a failure to share or link information within the system, particularly within the hospital and between the hospital and the community services.

Having first met in March 1995, our work was more or less completed by October of that year. However, the report didn't see the light of day until August 1998, when it was eventually published. The inquiry was suspended following legal proceedings brought by the children against the health board and the family's general practitioner. Sophia McColgan, the eldest girl, who waived her anonymity, had already spent two days in the witness box in the criminal trial. It galled me, knowing what I knew, that the children were being put through another ordeal when the facts of the matter had been well established. As could be seen in the more recent cervical screening debacle in 2018, insurance underwriting and organisational protection can sometimes appear to take precedence over a statutory organisation's primary duty of care to individuals. The hearing in the civil case went on for thirteen days over almost two months before a settlement was finally reached. Each of the children received a substantial payment and had their legal costs met, but there was no admission of liability.

*

In the decade or so between the Sligo and Roscommon inquiries, the child care landscape had changed utterly. The old health boards were gone, replaced by the monolithic Health Service Executive (HSE). More robust management structures were in place and there were considerably more social workers and other family support staff. National guidelines for the protection and welfare of children were introduced by the Department of Health and Children in 1999. The following year, the same department launched a National Children's Strategy. In 2007, the Health Information and Quality Authority (HIQA) was established, charged with regulating and monitoring health and social services. Sexual abuse had become a more common form of reported child abuse than physical abuse, so there was a high level of professional awareness.

In January 2009, a Roscommon mother of six was sentenced to seven years in jail for incest, neglect and ill treatment in relation to her own children. She would also be the first woman to be placed on the Sex Offenders Register upon her release. The judge commented that the children had been failed by everyone. She noted that, although the Western Health Board was involved with the family since 1996, the children were not being taken into care until 2004. During her trial, the mother described hers as the 'House of Horrors'. This was God's gift to the media and the title stuck.

Hanged If You Do...

I was sitting in my office in Swords, where I worked as a national child care specialist, when I had an unannounced visit from a senior national manager. She didn't come in but stood in the doorway holding a sheaf of papers disdainfully between her forefinger and thumb, as if she was looking to dispose of a dead mouse. The papers turned out to be a preliminary report on Roscommon, which she had ordered following the barrage of publicity. She said she was setting up an inquiry team and asked me to join it. As with Sligo, I agreed on the spot. The chairperson was to be Norah Gibbons, then director of advocacy in Barnardos. The other members were Leonie Lunny, former chief executive of the Citizens Information Board, and Gerry O'Neill, a national HSE manager with special responsibility for child care.

As soon as the inquiry team was announced, there was uproar in the Dáil and in the media about the independence of the inquiry team, given the membership of two HSE officials. Alan Shatter TD called for an independent commission to be established, pursuant to the Commission of Investigation Act 2004. While the charge of the HSE investigating itself was understandable on one level, the social worker in me felt very aggrieved at having my name out there in the media as someone incapable of reaching independent professional conclusions. By this time, I had conducted many reviews and investigations and there were many HSE staff on the receiving end who could vouch that I was well able to call a spade a spade. On 27 January 2009, Barry Andrews, Minister of State for Children and Youth Affairs, addressed the issue in the Dáil. He said he had every confidence in Norah Gibbons as chair to get to the full facts of the matter. He welcomed comments from Fergus Finlay, chief executive of Barnardos, on RTE radio that he did not believe there could be any possible vested interest in covering up the truth. He said, having met myself and Gerry O'Neill on several occasions, he fully endorsed these remarks.

When the inquiry started in February 2009, matters were *sub judice* because there was an outstanding criminal case in relation to the father which had not yet been heard. Then, in March 2010, he was sentenced to fourteen years for the rape and assault of his children. With the blaze of publicity surrounding each trial, we were acutely aware of the children's right to privacy and the need to shield them as much as possible from the media's duty to report the news. We were conscious too that further publicity would inevitably follow with the publication of the report.

As the inquiry team, we based ourselves in the Hodson Bay Hotel on Lough Rea, a stone's throw from Athlone, but nevertheless in County Roscommon. We were such frequent guests that on more than one occasion I was mistaken for a member of staff. We were tasked with examining the entire management of the case and to identify any shortcomings in the care management process. Norah informally met four of the children, who were in foster care. They were too young to engage in the investigation in their own right and it would have been intrusive for the rest of us to bother them. However, from the outset, we put ourselves in the children's shoes and tried to view all experiences, events and interventions from their perspective.

We examined the period between 1989, when the first child was born, and 2004, when the children were taken into care. We found that the children were denied their most basic needs. Indicators of neglect included an absolutely squalid home environment, poor personal hygiene, inadequate clothing, being left alone while the parents were out drinking and a complete absence of any family routine. The children literally lived from hand to mouth. On top of all this, they were abused by their parents in their own home where they had every right to feel safe and secure.

As in Sligo, we had no powers to compel people to meet us, yet most came willingly. Over the course of the inquiry we met thirty-eight witnesses. Only one person, a social worker no longer employed by the HSE, declined to attend. A whole range of professionals were engaged with the family over the years – social workers, public health nurses, child care workers, area medical officers, home helps, home care advisory workers, community welfare officers, psychologists, childcare managers and GPs. However, to a large extent, there was a lack of coordination with individuals working in their own silos. Most of the people we met were genuinely upset about what happened. But despite their good intentions, there was a failure to identify the extent and severity of the neglect and abuse suffered by each of these children from the time of their birth until their admission to care in 2004.

The Western Health Board was renowned for its well-developed family support services. This is due in no small measure to the ground-breaking work of Prof. Pat Dolan, current director of the UNESCO Child and Family Research Centre, National University of Ireland Galway, and former social care worker in the Western Health Board. Ironically, one of our main findings in this case was that the local staff had developed a default position whereby family support was pursued as the primary intervention even when it wasn't working. With this mindset, staff were not sufficiently alert to the child protection needs of the children who, in the end, had to rescue themselves.

When the report issued, with severe criticism of the former health board and its staff's involvement in the case, there wasn't a mention of our independence in the Dáil or in the media. On the day of publication, the HSE issued a statement saying that it accepted in full the findings and recommendations. More importantly, unlike Sligo, it issued a public apology to the six children.

*

In advance of any big case review it is possible, with a reasonable degree of certainty, to put the main findings in a sealed envelope before it starts and to be right when the envelope is opened at the end. Invariably, serious case reviews expose deficiencies in individual assessments, where the facts were not adequately elicited or seen for what they were. There will be a lack of inter-agency cooperation as well as a lack of intra-agency cooperation. But if these issues were easy to rectify, they would not be repeated ad nauseam. The context in which the casework takes place is as important as the casework itself. There is a public expectation that social workers should get it right all of the time. While that is desirable in principle, it is not attainable in practice because child protection is not susceptible to scientific law. At best, it is based on predictions derived from past behaviour as to the likelihood of future harm. At worst it is a response to the unpredictable behaviour where harm has already occurred.

In 2009, the Report of the Commission to Inquire into Child Abuse (Ryan Report) recommended that HIQA should develop guidance for the conduct of reviews of serious incidents including the deaths of children in State care. Consequently, in 2010, HIQA did just that. Its guidance said that a standardised, independent and transparent system for review should be introduced. It also prescribed that a national panel be established, with an independent chair and a range of suitable professionals. Within the HSE, I was charged with setting up the National Review Panel (NRP). Dr Helen Buckley, then associate professor in the School of Social Work and Social Policy, Trinity College Dublin, was appointed as the independent chair. In this capacity, she brought great rigour and expertise, as well as independence.

As is typical in bureaucracies, all the organisational emphasis went into being able to announce that a review panel was established. Where it might be based and how it would be administered and funded were mere details. When I approached the relevant national director about the need for an office manager I was told, 'Just find someone and take them.' I knew that poaching was not a way to win friends and influence people – but with some good fortune and the assistance of a colleague, a senior administrator who was looking for a change was identified. Ann Kennedy and I met in Dr Steeven's hospital and, having sounded each other out, we both decided to take a chance on each other. For eight subsequent years, until her retirement in 2018, Ann was the backbone of the NRP.

After prolonged cajoling of an elusive Estates Management Department, we were offered offices in Fenian Street, Dublin. The space was adequate and we were assured that there would be connectivity to the HSE computer network. Even though

I was somewhat apprehensive about the sign in the lift which read 'Do not use if you are the last person to leave the building', I took the keys. They were tossed into my hand, like a scrap to a dog, then an estate manager announced that, by the way, the lease on the building was to expire in a few months. And the communications issues were never resolved. Against the odds we pulled it off and a National Review Panel of high standing was established, thanks to the calibre of the members who joined it.

Under Helen Buckley's leadership, a standardised approach to case reviews was developed and introduced. Several years on, clear themes have emerged from the work of the NRP. Echoing the findings in the Roscommon report, the NRP frequently finds that neglect is a primary source of concern; there is a high incidence of parental alcohol and drug abuse; the initial assessment is often too superficial and not revised to take account of changing circumstances; cases tend to be categorised as a welfare concern instead of the more serious child protection concern, thereby receiving a less intensive response than required; risks are not always recognised; and focus is placed on the capacity of the parent to perform certain tasks rather than considering their actual behaviour, which may be the cause of the harm.

In approaching any case review, the reviewer would do well to approach the task with a modicum of humility. For one thing, no one knows the day nor the hour when the tables might be turned and their work will be meticulously scrutinised. Furthermore, child protection social work is the management of uncertainty, not the prediction of certainty. Reviewing, as opposed to doing, always has the incalculable benefit of hindsight.

17

Red Tape

I was interviewing social workers for some mid-management post or other. In an attempt to get away from the habitual 'woe is me' depiction of social work, I asked each candidate if they could describe an action they recently took that made them proud of being a social worker. One, heaving a sigh of the condemned, lowered his chin and uttered, 'Jaysus, you have me there.' Another was his antithesis, declaring with unfettered pride that he had just reported his employer to HIQA for a breach of national standards. Mindful that a Trump-like reaction to whistleblowing might not be the thing from a senior manager in an interview setting, I tentatively queried how that action fitted with his loyalty to his employer who, after all, lodged money into his bank account every month. 'My loyalty is to my profession,' he scowled. This provides a parable for the conflicted loyalty social workers often have between their profession and their agency.

Social workers are trained to be champions for social justice and advocates for service users. They are bound to be, according to their code of ethics – but this loyalty to the client can lead to conundrums. In child protection work, where there is usually a hypothesis that there is a victim and a perpetrator, social work empathy tends to be stuck on the pro-victim side of the good guy/bad guy dial. But, as in any investigative process, the social worker's assessment must follow the evidence and not the heart. This is done by hearing both sides of the story, seeking any available corroborative evidence, making an analysis of the facts, and drawing a conclusion based on the balance of probability. Despite their training, ethics and instinct, social workers must afford the accused person due process in order to comply with the basic laws of natural justice.

This quest for what lawyers call 'fair procedures' has led to all sorts of politically correct processes and parlance. Victims become 'alleged victims' or 'complainants' while perpetrators (never perps) become 'alleged perpetrators', or 'persons subject of abuse allegations' (PSAAs). I was once at a meeting with a PSAA who was legally represented. We deftly pirouetted around the terminology as I set out what I thought was the compelling evidence of the alleged victim. Then the advocate for the accused, momentarily tripping over the language, blurted, 'That's all very well for the alleged victim, but what about the alligator?'

As with other professional groups, social workers possess a central value system that is shared by them alone. It is often accompanied by a language than only they know, and this adds to the mystification of the professional clique. I once eavesdropped on two doctors whom I was sitting behind on the train. One was describing a tricky presentation to the other, but their rapid descent into clinical language spoiled the voyeuristic effect and I eventually lost all interest.

Laws set out what is to be done but they are broadly silent on how it is to be done. Consequently, social workers develop their own way of doing things – cases get opened, processed and closed. In undertaking this work, professional elitism renders social workers resistant to bureaucratic oversight and control, like cockroaches to pesticide. Professional supervision by fellow social workers is an acceptable form of regulation but diktats from administrators are not. Like that job interviewee, their primary loyalty is to their profession, not their employer. And being trained to look out for the interests of clients, they are less concerned about views of other stakeholders.

When an organisation has a culture that is broadly shared by all within it, there is likely to be a shared vision as to what they are all trying to achieve. The organisational mission is clear and agreed. My father was an army officer. Every year he attended a religious retreat held in the barracks – some time-out for reflection and contemplation. Then the brass had a thought: 'Hang on. This is the army – we can't retreat.' The problem was solved when the chaplain cleverly rebranded the event as a mission.

Simple uni-functional organisations, a children's charity for example, are most likely to have a mission that is well understood and agreed by all staff. Large complex organisations, however, will not and are likely have a convoluted organisational structure reflecting its multi-functional nature. The story goes that a new chief executive for the HSE asked what the line of command was between him and a porter in a general hospital. He was told that a working party would be formed forthwith to look into it.

A classic indicator that an organisation is a bureaucracy is when each part of it works in isolation from the other, is entirely self-serving and is disconnected from the organisational mission. It is like a hapless moose – its body is disproportionately large and its brain is disproportionately small. Like a moose trying to cross a frozen lake, its legs are likely to slide in unintended directions beyond the control of the brain. For practitioners, the four legs of bureaucracy are policy, HR, finance and technical support. The operators will have assessed the risk and know that they want to cross the frozen water – but policy will have mapped out a different direction, HR will not authorise the deployment, finance will pull the plug midway across and technical support will log your call with a promise to get back you back as soon as possible. Your call is important to them. Then when the beast, exhausted by involuntary contortions, slips through the thin ice into torpor and eventual oblivion, quality assurance will arrive. It will dispassionately review the event, pointing out how things went wrong and how it could all have been avoided.

Hanged If You Do...

While it is sometimes tempting, even satisfying, to consider justifiable homicide when dealing with bureaucracy, it is worth remembering that the transaction isn't personal. The system is both impervious and indifferent to your anger, your upset and your predicament. Its psychopathic nature is without mercy and may indeed take some passing pleasure in your pain. Being egocentric, it knows it is always right. This may occasionally be disguised in chirpy, patronising customer service speak.

I once bought a new computer that turned out to be faulty. On my first call to customer support, a saccharine voice assured that only my ignorance was at fault and to follow the online guidance, which was foolproof. My second call to customer support diagnosed a software problem. My third call to customer support diagnosed a hardware problem. My fourth call to customer support prompted the suggestion, all else having failed, to turn it off and on again. My fifth call to customer support did not get me the conversation I requested with a manager, but I was promised a call back. Time passed. Then one day their number came up on my telephone screen, and, in my rush to pick up, I kicked over a table in a coffee house. When I pressed 'receive' a robotic but decidedly cheerful voice simpered, 'Hello! You missed a call from us. Goodbye.'

My first encounter with 'the system' came when I went to claim my first pay cheque. Having signed a contract, I turned up at a designed time and place to apply my marketable skills as a social worker in return for an agreed level of remuneration. I was to be paid every fortnight. Two weeks passed but there was no sign of any payment. Then another two and another two. After a series of phone calls to various pay centres I eventually found someone who would at least acknowledge that I was an employee. Then he asked, 'What's the problem anyway?' Are you in a hurry for it?' Apart for having just bought a house and being weeks away from getting married, I was in no hurry at all.

When I took up my first management job in the mid-1980s, I had no clerical support. There was a secretary based several miles away who was shared by the whole team of seventeen social workers. In the age before computers, if I wanted a letter typed I had to drive to the secretary with my handwritten version and back again the following day to pick up the typed version. This went on for years, but then along came the fax machine – it was cutting-edge technology. Like a boy with his nose against a sweetshop window, I really wanted one. I made a case to the relevant administrator, pointing out that it would save time to fax my documents to the secretary rather than driving them to and from her. 'Why would it?' he asked. 'It's only your time that's getting lost.' Down but not out, I switched tack, arguing that it would save money as well because I was claiming a milage allowance for the journeys to and fro. He wavered, but then proclaimed, 'The doctors don't even have one.' In one last-ditch effort, I offered to share the machine with the doctors. That sealed it – fax machines were installed at the sending and receiving ends. But the administrator was at pains to point out, firstly, that they were the property of the administration, not the social workers and, secondly, this was only a trial. Written conditions were imposed whereby there would be a full cost benefit analysis on the use of the facsimile machines after a reasonable period of time. I am pleased to say I'm still waiting for the results.

It was the late 1990s before I got my own office computer and well into the new millennium before I was set up for the internet. Technical services doled it out like it was on prescription. There was much questioning as to why I wanted to use it and how I managed up until now. I pointed out that the same could have been asked about making fire. Various levels of access were permitted, depending on one's grade and function. As I was then in a policy role, access to online research seemed like a no-brainer. Eventually a gushing email from technical services advised that they had bestowed me access to the world wide web. To get myself started, I typed in 'Department of Health'. Instantly a message flashed angrily on the screen, 'Access denied. Reason – leisure activity'. So I tried 'children's services'. That was a big mistake – the thought police got the wrong idea altogether and my access was completely withdrawn. This was followed by a full-scale investigation into my thirty-second search history.

Hanged If You Do...

Form-filling is the lot of an employee within a bureaucracy and it's not made any easier now that much of it is online. I recently did a job for a public service organisation. I filled in the forms, just as I had done for other sections within the same organisation, but, no, each section had their own way of doing things. I submitted an invoice with a separate electronic form for a mileage claim. But it was a yellow form and it should have been a green one. I submitted the green one to be told it should have been yellow all along. It then transpired that the yellow form was possessed by electronic gremlins who contorted any date combination I entered. So 20/9/19 became 9/20/19, and 200919 became 092019 and so on. If I slowly, surreptitiously, edged the cursor towards a number and backspaced quickly it would sometimes correct itself for a fleeting moment. But it would always revert to a non-existent date as soon as my back was turned. In the end, I printed out a blank form and filled it in by hand. I submitted this as an email attachment, but the organisation's firewall considered it suspect and consigned it to cyberspace.

A great yardstick for measuring the way organisations present themselves to the outside world is their reception area. It is the front door to their world. I once brought a Danish delegation to a service for homeless adults. Outside a locked front door an orderly queue of bedraggled people lined up. I rang the bell. Twice. An irritated and groggy porter, who sounded like he had been roused from the sleep of the dead, eventually opened a sash window behind a security grill yelling, 'Yes! What?' One of the Danes asked me, 'This is the way you greet the public?'

I travel around the country a lot these days doing business with voluntary and statutory social services. Warm, friendly receptionists really make the front-of-house experience. Elsewhere I have been confronted by indifferent grumps behind glass windows who seemed trained in the tactics of belittlement. 'What's the name of your child,' one grump asked me. When I said I wasn't here about a child she snorted, 'Then what are you doing here?' Elsewhere there is a sign on an ancient wooden door which says, 'For social workers, ring bell.' Except it would seem you have to bring your own bell. Then there is the public building where the public are locked out altogether. Instead of a reception there is a sign instructing people to phone the person they came to see.

When you do make it to the reception area, there are, almost without exception, posters laying down the law around conduct. For example, 'Please keep your children under control.' If they could do that, they would probably not be queuing up to see the social worker in the first place. Other signs telling people not to be aggressive are in themselves inherently aggressive. If you were to escape to the toilets to bang your head in frustration against the wall, you would be hard-pressed to find a vacant sliver of space that is not itself covered in more warnings: 'Don't forget to wash your hands.' 'Caution - hot water may be hot', and (perish the thought), 'Leave these toilets the way you found them.'

Years ago I was passing through a health centre when I noticed one of the country's most senior managers sitting in a queue between the dental and the child health clinics. When I asked him what he was doing he said, 'Observing - just making sure things are working.' Bring back old-style public service!

18

The Divorce

'*T*ell me your story', was the first thing the new boss, Gordon Jeyes, ever said to me. Moments earlier he had walked ahead of me from the general office to his. There was no handshake, no introductory pleasantries – just a sideways glance, then a nod from his PA to follow him. As he walked in front, I traipsed behind, feeling like newly purchased bullock at a farmers' mart.

This was February 2011 and Gordon was the newly appointed National Director of Child Care Services in the HSE. He arrived in a blizzard to Ireland's child care services, which were going through their own winter of discontent. Prior to his appointment, child care had always been the poor relation of the health service – a barnacle on the backside of a health service whale. But a period of bad publicity resulted in a Government-prompted decision by the HSE to create a new position, National Director of Child Care Services, to give it the attention and management expertise it badly needed.

When Gordon started in the HSE, I was working away from the action in a remote corner where the phone seldom rang. It was a self-imposed exile as a consequence of my disgruntlement with previous national management arrangements. But soon after that meeting with Gordon, I moved into his offices and back into the thick of things, joining a tiny and disparate group of professionals and administrators who sat on pods in a leaky, open-plan office outside his.

From the mid-2000s, the HSE child care services, and child protection in particular, were getting a lot of negative public attention. The HSE commissioned an independent consultant to prepare a report on the life and death of a teenager who had been well-known to the child protection and care services throughout her life. It was completed in 2008 but never published, causing media and political eyebrows to raise in wonder as to what was not being made public.

There was mounting political concern regarding the likelihood of other cases concerning the death of children within the care system. In March 2010, the HSE told the Public Accounts Committee that twenty children known to its care and protection services had died over the last decade. The figure was subsequently found to be a gross underestimate, leading to a public perception that the HSE was so callous that it had not even bothered to collate the number of the children who died in its care or under its supervision.

The commissioned report leaked. Then Alan Shatter, an opposition TD, placed it on the Dáil record, effectively publishing it. The previous year he had disclosed the girl's name in the context of a Dáil debate – the report itself only had her initials. In relation to this particular girl, he correctly pointed out that, although she died in 2002 of a drug overdose, a review was not completed until the end of 2008, after which it did not see the light of day for a further two years. The report was very critical of the services provided, describing it as a chaotic response which went nowhere near meeting her needs.

Barry Andrews, Minister of State for Children and Youth Affairs, was on the back foot. In March 2010, he established an Independent Child Death Review Group (ICDRG) co-chaired by Dr Geoffrey Shannon, a leading authority on child and family law and the Government's Special Rapporteur on Child Protection, and Norah Gibbons, director of advocacy in Barnardos, an outspoken advocate for children. They examined the deaths of children in care, aftercare or known to child protection services between 2000 and 2010.

The ICDRG reported in June 2012. It identified 196 deaths across the three categories; 86 of which were from natural causes. Of the 112 deaths by unnatural causes, drugs, suicide and road traffic accidents were the most frequent causes. The review also highlighted prevalent issues within the homes of the young people who died, including neglect, drug and alcohol misuse, physical and sexual abuse, and child behavioural problems. The report concluded that the majority of the children who died had not received adequate protection from the services dedicated to that purpose.

Weeks after Gordon Jeyes took up his position as National Director, there was a general election. The new Taoiseach, Enda Kenny, appointed Francis Fitzgerald as the first full cabinet Minister for Children and Youth Affairs. The Programme for Government 2011-2016 committed to reforming child protection by removing it from the HSE and to establishing a new children's agency with improved accountability to the Dáil.

Frances Fitzgerald set up a task force for the establishment of a new Child and Family Agency, which reported in July 2012. It advocated for an agency with a broad base of family support services. The child protection element of the HSE was to be merged with the functions of the Family Support Agency and the National Educational Welfare Board, thereby extending the remit of the new agency beyond child protection. Frances Fitzgerald appointed Norah Gibbons as the first chairperson of the board. She was a widely popular choice as an independent children's champion. The Minister appointed Gordon Jeyes to be the chief executive of the new Child and Family Agency and the work on recruiting the rest of the management team commenced.

I applied for, and got, the job of Director of Policy and Strategy. An essential requirement for the post was a professional qualification in social work, and it was the only position on the national management team to require one. By the time of my appointment, it was towards the end of 2012 and the Agency was supposed to go live at the beginning of 2013. Other key management posts had been not filled by the end of that year, and there was so much to be done to disentangle children's services from the HSE. There were budgets to be set, and we were still dependent on the HSE in critical areas such as payroll, estate management and computer support. The HSE, like an estranged spouse, held on tightly to the purse strings. The divorce which followed, separating child care from the HSE, was an acrimonious one where they got the money and we got the children.

In the end, the Minister put back the establishment date until 1 January 2014, and even then it was a white-knuckle ride to get the basics over the line in time. Throughout this count-down period, we operated as a shadow management team for the Agency. Most of us were still technically part of the HSE, with others coming from the outside.

There was a lot of coming and going of senior staff during this period. Some people, who were not successful at interview for jobs on the management team, shuffled off. Others just couldn't hack it with Gordon, or he with them. I was reminded of that old book by Dale Carnegie, *How to Win Friends and Influence People,* and soon formed the opinion that Gordon had not taken a leaf from that book. He could influence people – of that there was no doubt. He was at his best on his feet, reeling in an audience. But at an individual level he hadn't come to Ireland to win friends – and he wasn't bothered about people needing to feel the love. To paraphrase Peter Drucker, the management guru, good intentions don't move mountains, bulldozers do. And there were an awful lot of mountains.

We all knew we had been gifted a once-in-a-career oppor-tunity to determine the culture of a brand-new organisation that would set the tone for years to come. The prospect was as exciting as it was daunting. There was a lot for ground to make up following the HSE's calamitous reputation, renowned for circling the wagons when confronted by public scrutiny. To set a new tone, we boiled down our approach to three words – accountability, consistency and transparency.

And so began the hard slog of winning hearts and minds. Gordon had come from the UK system where, by and large, people did what they were told. Therefore, he was at once flabbergasted and exasperated at the rebel nature of the Irish, who put up epic local resistance from strongholds throughout the country. It wasn't that people were not prepared to change – it was that they didn't want to be told by that crowd up in Dublin that they had to. Effective change management has three essential requisites – consult, consult, consult. So we hit the road.

By the time the Child and Family Agency went live on 1 January 2014, a lot of groundwork had been done with staff and key stakeholders. We were determined to do things differently – ensuring staff shared the vision and that children and families had a meaningful say in how services were developed and run. The reorganisation created a clear line of sight from the chief executive to the people knocking on doors to deliver the service. If we had learned anything from the HSE, it was that convoluted, top-heavy management structures don't work. The country was divided into seventeen areas. Each area would be run by an area manager who had responsibility for everything – budget, staff, funded services, performance, the lot. The areas were then rolled up into four regions which were managed by service directors. The idea was that the regional offices would be a sub-branch of the national office, which would then have close oversight of what was happening at street level. But from an early stage local loyalty stopped at the regional office. A 'them and us' quickly emerged where the regional jersey was worn with pride but the national colours were reserved for the people in the Dublin headquarters.

In reality, we kept things really lean in the HQ. I had considerably less administrative support than any of the area managers or service directors. When I was first appointed to the national management team, I had no administrative support at all. I then shared a PA with another director before eventually getting a full-time person to myself.

The Department of Children and Youth Affairs (DCYA) were naturally all over us during the lead-up to the establishment of the Agency, and they shared our determination and worked hard to seize the opportunity to make radical and meaningful changes in the delivery of children's services. At one stage, before the Agency went live, the DCYA hosted a meeting between the Department of Health, the HSE management team and our incoming management team. It was co-chaired by the secretaries general, who were essentially there to mediate an ongoing row about money. Two things stood out for me at that meeting. The first was that I didn't recognise many of the HSE faces, such was the turnover on their management team. The second was that the leader of the HSE delegation got up and left after fifteen minutes. It wasn't a walk-out – they just had something more pressing to do than assisting two Government departments in setting up a new agency for Ireland's children.

Because those in the Department of Children and Youth Affairs were as anxious as we were to deliver a first-class service, they operated a 'man-marking' system when the Agency went live. Particular civil servants were assigned to monitor particular directorates. Minister Fitzgerald, with her background in social work, was no pushover either and was well able to interrogate the data, and us. Even though it was by any standards a small Department, there were a lot more of them than there was of us. We had to attend torturous monthly meetings where every tiny detail would be picked over. On arrival, we would be greeted by a row of highly prepared civil servants, flexing their muscles like athletes at a starting line. At the time we were already working day and night to get the Agency off to a good start, but we understood that the Department also had a stake in the action. Still, we might have all done better if we pooled our limited resources a bit more.

For the first while we got a fair wind from the media and the usual suspects in the voluntary sector who liked to criticise statutory services from the sideline. There was a recognition among critics and observers that adequate resourcing of the new Agency was a major factor. Despite that, we committed to live within our means even if this limited our output in key service delivery areas. As time went on, people were more disposed to finding fault in the light of endless HIQA reports, case reviews, inspections, court cases, Dáil committees and so on as the day-to-day work continued.

As part of the transformation process, the Agency dealt with the voluntary sector not as charities but as the commissioned services they were. After all, there was nothing charitable about their payroll. Some of the voluntary organisations became discontented, feeling that they had been repositioned as service providers rather than partners. Nevertheless, the board of the Child and Family Agency brought great credibility to the Agency. Under the strict chairmanship of Norah Gibbons, who had worked in the voluntary sector, integrity and strong governance was assured.

I retired in the middle of 2015. I could have stayed on for another few years, but the Agency was up and running and it seemed like a good idea for me to do the same. Being a central part of the establishment of Ireland's first agency dedicated to the welfare and protection of children was a fairy-tale ending to my career. I wondered how I would feel on the last day, as a sense of loneliness set in. But when the day came, the overall feeling was one of contentment. Just as the lift reached the ground floor of our new headquarters and I was making my exit, I got a text from someone asking me when I was retiring. 'I just have', I replied.

In December 2018, I went back to the headquarters to attend a farewell celebration for Norah Gibbons, whose tenure of office had come to an end. The Agency was by then on its third chief executive in only five years. Stepping into the lift, I was amazed to find that they had acquired seven additional floors. One floor for each year since just ten of us sat at pods in an open-plan office within a rickety HSE building, following Gordon Jeyes' arrival. I had to ask, and still wonder, 'what do all these people do?'

19

Hanged If You Do....

A colleague of mine had images of social workers which she used in presentations. First, she would show a social worker who took a child into care. The image was a cartoon of a matchstick man being hanged. Then she would show a cartoon of a social worker who did not take a child into care. It was the same image. When disaster strikes, social workers become the vessel for the outpouring of society's outrage. Public discourse shifts from what the perpetrator did to what the social workers did, or did not, do. Then this becomes the story.

All of the major non-statutory inquiries held to date serve as examples of being hanged for sins of omission. The Kilkenny Incest Report (1993), the West of Ireland Farmer (1998), Monageer (2009) and the Roscommon Child Care Case (2010) all highlight how services failed to intervene with sufficient effectiveness in individual child protection cases. Following the publication of each of these inquiry reports, the media asked the inevitable questions, how could it have happened and who will be held accountable?

Then in 2013, there was the bizarre case of the Roma children where service providers were hanged for what they did. The Gardaí and social workers were severely criticised for being overzealous by removing children from their families without sufficient grounds. It followed the discovery of a blond-haired, blue-eyed girl in a Roma camp in Greece which made world news. Soon after, the Gardaí were alerted to the presence of a blond-haired child in a Roma family in Tallaght. Suspicious that the seven-year-old girl had been abducted, the gardaí removed the child under emergency powers and placed her in the care of the HSE. The child was held in care by the HSE until DNA tests confirmed the child belonged in the family from which she had been removed.

To compound matters, on the very next day in Athlone, gardaí removed a two-year-old blond-haired Roma boy from his family despite the fact that the parents produced identification papers for him. He was placed in an out-of-hours foster home. The following morning, when the professionals who knew him came to work, they vouched for his identity and he was allowed home. Alan Shatter TD, Minister for Justice and Equality, commissioned Ms Emily Logan, Ombudsman for Children, to conduct an inquiry and produce a report on the matter. She concluded that, in both cases, ethnic profiling was a big contributory factor in the decisions to remove the two children from their families. Although the Gardaí probably came out worse than the social workers, the report was described in the media as a wakeup call for the child protection system.

*

An early example of a personal public lynching occurred in 1996. On 16 March, Fr Peter McVerry, the Jesuit priest who campaigns for and ministers to the homeless, wrote a letter to the *Irish Times*. He had a go at the Eastern Health Board concerning some young people he knew who were, or had been, in the care of that health board. At the time, I was the relatively new Director of Child Care and Family Support Services in the Eastern Health Board. I took Fr McVerry on by writing to the *Irish Times* countering his claims. I said it was incorrect to suggest that social workers were not in touch with a fifteen-year-old whose placement broke down. They were actually in contact with him all the time. And it was a cheap shot to suggest that we didn't care if the youth was dead or alive. I went on to refute his other claim that a twelve-year-old boy had been placed in a B&B and was on the street by day with no food. I pointed out that he was, in fact, in a new, fully staffed residential centre in a premises that used to be a B&B. No sooner had I sat back in satisfaction at seeing my letter in print than the phone rang. It was RTE television.

For the next week or so, I had a nerve-wrecking path worn to a variety of television studios doing live TV head-to-head encounters with Peter McVerry. The story gobbled airtime. This encounter taught me two valuable lessons. One, thinking you are right does not necessarily mean that you will be believed. And two, never wrestle a living saint – it's unseemly.

Most people become social workers for well-motivated, altruistic reasons. Those social workers who go into child protection do a dirty job of society that is not without a personal cost. Vicarious trauma is an occupational hazard. And it is the statutory sector that does all the heavy lifting in child protection. It came as a shock to me, therefore, when the penny finally dropped that working in the statutory sector casts you in the role of villain, despite all those heroic intentions and noble deeds. So there I was in a television studio explaining how I was right and the priest was wrong. The typecasting was so stereotypical that I might as well have strangled a puppy, live on air. I would have had a better chance as an interviewee in the Spanish Inquisition. Managing the message, I learned, requires more than just the truth. It also requires choreography, cunning and courage – all of which I lacked back then.

*

When it comes to reporting child protection stories, good news is no news. Creative initiatives or proactive measures get little or no media coverage. Stories are selected for their sensational value. For five years, I briefed the media on reports of serious incidents or deaths involving children known to the State or child protection services, or who were in State care. This was required under the guidance issued by the Health

Hanged If You Do...

Information and Quality Authority. The reports were prepared by the National Review Panel, an independent body established to undertake investigations of each incident and to prepare a report on them.

Under the auspices of the Health Service Executive, and the Child and Family Agency from its establishment in 2014, we organised an annual press conference to present the data to the media. I fronted for the Agency, and Dr Helen Buckley, from the School of Social Work and Social Policy, spoke for the National Review Panel. The most common cause of death of cases known to the child protection services is natural causes, followed by suicide and road traffic accidents. Most of them were not in care. Despite these facts, presented to the media in advance of the launch, the headlines invariably had a sensational twist, such as, 'Twenty-three children die in State care.'

The fact that most were not in care and died from natural causes was a detail. It was always made to read and sound like we had a firing squad on standby out the back. The story would usually run from early morning as a headline story on the radio, hours before the press conference even commenced. I would spend the rest of the day running after the story in an attempt to achieve some balance. But, as they say, when you're explaining, you're losing. It wasn't as if the child protection service always covered itself in glory – there was plenty of factual material there to report upon. Spokespersons for the larger voluntary organisations would then be invited by the media to cast stones. And always the key questions were: were these deaths preventable and is someone going to be held accountable?

Like the media, voluntary organisations are in the fortunate position of being able to comment upon the shortcomings of the statutory sector without fear of the spotlight falling on their own efficiency and effectiveness. In the public relations world, voluntary is good, statutory is bad. Voluntary organisations also get to pick and choose their work. With very little exception, this will be on the softer end of the spectrum, leaving the child protection duties to the statutory sector, which has ultimate responsibility for it. Sometimes there seems to be an incompatibility between what they say they do in fundraising messages and what the actually do in practice. I once worked with an organisation which supports homeless teenagers. A truculent teenager was placed in residential care with them. They eventually kicked him out, leaving the health board social workers holding the baby, so to speak. Then they shamelessly issued a press release saying what an outrage it was that there were insufficient services for troubled teens, as they reverted back to looking after the easy ones.

Only sensational child protection stories get published, such as ones with tragic outcomes, high-profile court cases involving abused children, or serious shortcomings in the child protection system itself. As such, there is a distortion in the media coverage because the more routine issues of neglect, parental addiction or domestic violence do not receive proportionate attention. A television journalist once said to me, 'It's my job to hold you to account.' I replied, more in surprise than annoyance, 'But I thought it was to report the news.' I already had a chief executive, a board, a Government Department, a Minister, HIQA, the Ombudsman for Children, the Ombudsman and the courts to hold me to account, so I was genuinely surprised by her assertion.

The public ridicule of child protection services when something goes wrong has a direct knock-on effect on the political system. The Minister has to be seen to be doing something. This will usually entail an independent investigation and a report that will inevitably contain recommendations for policy and procedural changes. These changes will not replace anything. Instead, they will be stacked on top of an already wobbling pile of existing policy and procedure. Compliance to these new policies and procedures will be monitored by regulators, such as HIQA. The increased volume of rules makes it more likely for partitioners to violate them. These violations will then be reported upon and will become a new story in its own right.

*

Hanged If You Do...

What happens when a splendid new policy, well-researched, justified in its existence and written in plain English, hits the system? All too often, it is seen by social workers to be as relevant as a Christmas tree sale on St Stephen's Day. In the Child and Family Agency, Ireland's statutory child welfare and protection service, I had responsibility for policy and strategy. One of the biggest challenges was to develop consistency of practice so that customer experience in Donegal was even roughly the same as it was in Donnycarney. Individual social work teams had their own way of doing things and if improvement was proposed by senior management, especially if they were sitting behind a desk up in Dublin, it was likely to be met by heroic local resistance.

Gordon Jeyes, the first chief executive of the Child and Family Agency, took on an English consultant to help us. He came up with a practice handbook to help standardise how things were done. It seemed an odd initiative to me at the time – the embroidering of deckchairs on a liner's maiden voyage. But in retrospect maybe I too was suffering from social work inertia, because at least the handbook put practice and procedure between two covers for the first time. The consultant also devised a system for managing intake and the prioritisation of cases coming in the front door. This was called *Measuring the Pressure*. We refined it and introduced it as the first nationally consistent process for reporting social work activity. A guiding principle was that service users were entitled to a response that was consistent, efficient, effective and proportionate. For once and for all it nailed down what was coming in the front door and how it was prioritised.

But systems are only as good as their implementation. The Honourable Mr Justice Peter Charlton, chairman of the tribunal to inquire into protected disclosures concerning Garda Maurice McCabe, had something to say about *Measuring the Pressure* when he reported in 2018. He said that, with regard to Cavan/Monaghan, he heard inconsistent evidence about the system. Evidence diverged as to how less urgent cases were prioritised. According to some it was random; according to others it was a system. He said the evidence provided to him was most unimpressive. The tribunal was satisfied that there was a random allocation of files that could not be dignified by calling it a system.

Defensive practice is an unintended consequence of over-scrutiny. Social workers play it safe. So, if there has been an investigation into a shortfall in practice, there will be an inevitable increase in the number of cases designated as child abuse. The number of children coming into care will also go up. Professional judgement is stifled by hyper-regulation because social workers will reach for the rule book. And when the rules don't work, a common response is to make more rules.

Associated with regulation is the rise of managerialism, with a philosophy that says what gets measured gets done. Human services are being shoehorned into measurable concepts such as inputs, outputs and key performance indicators. Instead of focusing on quality of practice, there is an emphasis on administrative accountability. These quantitive measures are the manifestation of widget counting. They measure activity and shortfalls, but they do not address the fundamental question – is the service making a positive difference to people's lives? Wernher von Braun, the rocket scientist, said he could lick gravity but sometimes the paperwork was overwhelming. This perceived regulatory intrusion can be a deal-breaker for social workers. There is plenty of evidence to show that form-filling, more than threats of violence or traumatic events involving children, causes child protection social workers to leave.

I was centrally involved in producing the first corporate plan for the Child and Family Agency, covering the period 2014-2017. It is steeped in the language of linking strategic objectives to short-, medium- and long-term outputs, key performance indicators, identification of key risks, and implementation management. Having been out of the system for a while now, I look back on all that management speak and see it for what it really is – gobbledygook. At the time, I came across a cartoon by Fran, the business cartoonist. It depicts a huddle of stressed-out managers at a flip chart. On the chart there are references to strategic target monitoring, core client identification, management, budget reconciliation and refocusing.

Then one manager turns to the others and says, 'What do you think about forgetting the whole thing and just going back to trying to help people a bit?'